A THIEF IN THE STOREHOUSE

Ron Wood

The Battle over Money in the Church

A Thief in the Storehouse ©
Copyright 2018 by Ron Wood
Previous version - The Thief in the Storehouse ©
Copyright 1999-2017 by Ronald E. Wood

ISBN: 978-1984182746

All rights reserved. No part of this material may be reprinted, duplicated, copied, shared or quoted beyond fifty words for review purposes either electronically, by email, the internet, or in print without the express written consent of the author. The author asserts all rights of international ownership. This material is copyrighted.

10 9 8 7 6 5 4 3 2

A Thief in the Storehouse

Comments

"I keep thinking about what you wrote. Every pastor in America needs to have this (book) on their desk." FRED RUMSEY, United Methodist Pastor

"This is excellent writing - the best book on the subject I've read." EUNICE STONE, Assembly of God Pastor

"It has been my privilege to know Ron for many years. As a former Elder in our church for ten years in Colleyville, Ron distinguished himself by his effective teaching, his prophetic insights, and his mastery of God's word. He also has unique insights as a businessman and church planter. It is from this perspective of seeing his gifts in action that I whole-heartedly commend this book. What you are about to read is not milk, but meat; not a snack, but a meal. May all who read this material be like the good soil that produces fruit– 30, 60, or 100-fold. I pray that God will bless you as you read and that you will be able to teach others also."

CHRIS BADGER was Senior Vice President of Texas Independent Bank in Dallas, Texas, at the time, the nation's largest bankers' bank. His career includes decades of professional banking experience. He served as an elder in Metroplex Covenant Church where he chaired the finance committee, taught on biblical finances, and supervised the financial counseling ministry of the church. After serving as President of Premier Bank in Grapevine, Texas, Chris Badger is semi-retired and owns Clearview Consulting.

Contents

A Thief in the House	1
The War Over Money	5
God Is Not Stingy	32
Have God as a Friend	41
Tithes vs Offerings	49
A Covenant of Blessing	55
The Jericho Issue	60
Evicting the Thief	68
Honor God's Servants	82
An Apostolic Paradigm	94
Concluding Cautions	111
Seven Summary Statements	118
The Wages of an Apostle	122

A Thief in the House

THE FLORIDA SUNSHINE was brilliant out of a deep blue sky. I pulled my car in among the tall pines of my driveway with the stack of study papers on the seat beside me. They were freshly printed, hot off the press. I was excited at the study notes I had prepared. The thought occurred to me that the devil would not like what I was doing. Little did I know that I had inflamed an angry devil. I was about to be the object of his wrath.

With this study, I was bringing forth teaching that the tithe—the first ten percent of our income—was holy unto the Lord and that it was assigned by God to directly support his servants in the ministry.

Our study of this subject had taken on new significance as our church had grown. God had prospered the work under my ministry. Many people had turned to the Lord. His blessings were evident. Not only did the church have its best year in terms of income but, for the first time in its history, there was money left over in the bank.

What were we to do with the surplus? Build a new auditorium? That might be a good use. But an idea had been developing in my mind—to plant a new church. That's a form of corporate evangelism. I knew it would require finances.

I also knew the mentality of those who worked with me on the church board. They had grown up under congregational government, a traditional democratic system where the pastor had little to say about the finances of the church. "Leave the preaching to the pastor and the finances to the businessmen on the board." That's the old way of thinking in many evangelical churches.

God was challenging our preconceptions. We had begun to explore what the Bible had to say about money and the ministry. We had taken our church surplus the year before and had given away thousands of dollars as alms in our community.

In our study, we had seen that the tithe was holy to the Lord and not everyone was authorized to handle it. We had seen in the New Testament that elders[1] had responsibility for the finances of the church. We saw that apostles had laid down clear guidelines for handling church finances.

Because of these insights, I sensed we were on the verge of a breakthrough. I also sensed we were being tested as to whether we would submit our old opinions to fresh insights from the word of God.

When it comes to handling money in the church, everybody with a religious background already has their opinion. Unfortunately, opinions contrary to God's word can lead people into sin. Opinions can cause strife. Little did I know that the battle over the tithe would soon become

---

[1] Elders (plural) are mature church leaders *(presbuteros)* who shepherd the flock. They oversee house churches or a congregation under the supervision of the apostle who appointed them. See Acts 20:28, *et al.*

personal and painful.

As I pulled into the driveway, I was surprised to see a Sheriff's car parked beside my house. Out among the trees in the front yard stood my friend Ralph. He was a respected businessman, retired from the lumber industry where he had worked for many years. He was elder in my church. I rolled my window down and stopped my car beside him.

"Preacher, you've been robbed!" he said.

"Miss Lana discovered it and called me," he said in his soft southern drawl.

"I phoned the Sheriff and they're inside now looking for fingerprints."

My wife, returning home alone, had walked into our empty house thirty minutes earlier. She had discovered the typical robbery scene—everything dumped out, drawers scattered, clothing in disarray on the floor, our small dog cowering and trembling in the corner.

I made sure she was alright. I held her and thanked God that she had not walked in while the robbers were still there. A bold noon break-in; a smash and grab.

We counted our losses. Everything portable of any value was gone. Our television, the VCR, my computer, my wife's jewelry, my daughter's jewelry, the gun a police detective had given me. Numerous personal effects were missing, much of it irreplaceable: the gold pocket watch my Mom had given me, the wristwatch my Dad had given me, a lockbox with Lana's adoption certificate, our marriage license. Even my socks! Ransacked and looted, all during the brief time Lana was gone to lunch and I was away at the printers.

We felt violated as if our home had been raped. I was angry at the thieves who had done this. I began to realize that the timing of this robbery was not a coincidence. And I thought, was this how God feels when we rob Him? Does the Lord feel anger, disappointment; a sense of violation?

"Will a man rob God? Yet you are robbing Me! Yet you say, 'How have we robbed You?' In tithes and offerings." (Malachi 3:8)

The War Over Money

WHILE STUDYING GOD'S ownership of the tithe, I had been robbed. While preparing a position paper on its proper use, I had walked into a war zone. Satan, the god of this world, was angry with me. Apparently, I had touched a sensitive nerve. Why? Because I had uncovered a divine truth which threatened the devil's realm. This was amazing. I had hold of information so deadly that it infuriated the Master Thief into striking out at me personally.

Since that day, I have become increasingly convinced that there is a war concerning money. It is not a theoretical war—it is a real battle, and we're all involved in it.

Satan is under an illusion: he thinks he owns all the money in the world. But he's wrong. Whatever the devil may have, he stole it. Jesus said that the devil is a thief (John 10:10).

That statement by Jesus isn't an allegory about the devil's nature—it is an *exact* description of his true character. Just like a rattlesnake will bite you because that's his nature, so Satan will steal anything that is unguarded.

The devil is true to his nature. He will rob anyone if given an opportunity. To avoid being ripped off by Satan, Christians must discover the truth regarding money and its proper use.

The truth about money is found in the Bible. It says that God created the wealth of this world. The wealth of the world is here for God's people to use, not for the wicked to control. There is an end-time transfer of wealth underway from the wicked to the righteous.

God's kingdom increases when Christians prosper through diligence, wise investments, and creative enterprise. When Christians prosper, they capture the world's resources. They take back what the devil stole. They walk into more of their inheritance. God wants more Christians to be wealthy. God wants churches on a mission to have all they need to advance the gospel.

Listen: *God wants you to know the truth so that you can prosper!* The devil doesn't want you to read this book. The devil wants to keep you ignorant of the truth; poor, broke, frustrated, and miserable.

Like it or not, we are caught up in this conflict over money. We win the battle by obeying the Scriptures. Our lives may be assaulted by evil forces, but if we trust in God, we will overcome.

This truth about money and the battle which surrounds it is very real to me. After you read this book, it will become real to you as well. God's word will strip away the veil which clouds our thinking concerning financial matters.

Poverty is NOT God's Will

Evil forces seem to be growing. Cultural values seem to be eroding. There is an end-time battle underway. This battle is ultimately for the eternal souls of men and women. Jesus came to save sinners. The spiritual war around us is fought over the fate of eternal souls.

A Thief in the Storehouse

It takes power to win souls. The gospel is meant to be preached with power. Two things empower us to win more souls: Holy Spirit, who illuminates the truth of the gospel; and our financial resources, which equip and employ more preachers, pastors and missionaries. Therefore, this cosmic struggle to win souls is corporately contested and diabolically resisted in two major areas—the gifts of the Holy Spirit being received and utilized, and the wealth of believers being used by God's leaders, such as apostles.[2]

Power is the ability to do work. Power is important. The first type of power is the anointing. The second type of power is money. One is spiritual; the other is natural. These two areas of empowerment (anointing and money) are strongly contested by enemy forces.

What do I mean by the anointing? The anointing is spiritual energy—the gifts and callings of God—which are so essential for the church to complete the Great Commission (1 Cor. 12 & Acts 10:38). The anointing increases our power to fulfill the great commission, to take the ministry of Jesus to lost and suffering people. The anointing releases our ministry gifts, the tools of the trade that signify God's kingdom.

The second focus of conflict is material, especially over money. Make no mistake about it, *money represents power.* Whoever we invest with money is empowered in their mission. Give money to a godless media-mogul and he'll put on MTV, psychic hotlines, and Howard Stern on television, coming into a million homes. If we give Billy Graham a million dollars, he'll set up a satellite feed system to simultaneously preach the gospel to the poor of the nations

---

[2] Apostles, unlike pastors, are pioneers. They are missional, expansive, and act as fathers in the faith. They are concerned with growing the kingdom of God and the sphere of the gospel's reach. They plant more churches and train more workers for the harvest.

and see thousands of souls saved. Money empowers people with influence to fulfill their vision, whether for good or for evil. Therefore, money matters. Indeed, when sanctified for holy purposes, money can become a positive spiritual force.

Like nuclear energy, real power must be safeguarded. Power needs to be channeled in the river bed of truth. Therefore, doctrinal correctness is important. Likewise, which ministry we empower with our contributions is critical.

Financial freedom follows the discovery of biblical principles about the priorities and purposes of money in God's kingdom.

Evangelism costs money. Let's face it—a broke church can't take care of itself, much less take the gospel to the nations. The gospel is free, but sending workers, supporting church programs, providing outreach to the poor, building worship facilities, Bible colleges and classrooms, and maintaining major ministry operations takes money, and lots of it.

Thank God, the cross has sufficient power to cancel the curse of poverty. God is in the curse-canceling business. God wants us all to break out of poverty and start to prosper. Why? Because the only method God has for financing the fulfillment of the Great Commission is to prosper his people, to release them into the faith-filled joyous grace of abundant giving. That means you!

The devil would love to keep God's people poor. A poverty mentality cripples people and hinders churches. Poverty is a form of oppression. *It is not a mark of spirituality to be poor!* Poverty shames people. Poverty which continues from one generation to the next can be caused by a generational curse. The Bible teaches us that idolatry brings the curse of poverty and that such a curse can linger for many generations. A curse is an evil pronouncement that affects people in a negative way.

God's grace eliminates curses and deposits blessings instead. Blessings make for abundance while curses make for lack. Poverty is not a virtue. It is a miserable existence. Poverty robs people of self-respect. Poverty denies people their human dignity. Poverty is contrary to God's will.

This doesn't mean we can look down on people who are poor: quite the opposite. God has chosen the poor of this earth to be rich in faith. (see James 2:5) The poor often respond the quickest to the gospel. But poverty, whether due to circumstances of birth, or war, or economic turmoil, or personal sin, or foolish spending, is *not* a blessing.

God doesn't cause poverty—sin does. God is against deprivation and suffering. He is also against the ingrained welfare mentality that justifies poverty and dependency as a way of life.

God honors work and wants our labor to be rewarded. All honest work is good. There is no menial task when it is done for God's glory and our family's benefit. God is a rewarder and enjoys seeing us happy.

An attitude that expects to remain poor or that condones poverty makes way for a non-biblical deceit, a mental stronghold that resists God's truth. A stronghold is always based on a lie. Believing a lie produces oppression and leaves its victims in slavery. Thus, the origins of poverty are spiritual in nature and familial in effect. Poverty can run inter-generationally.

To tolerate poverty and to accept it as a normal condition means you have believed something that runs cross-grain to the Bible. Believing a lie sets us up for evil influences. Wrong doctrine makes room for deception. Wrong thinking, persistently believed, makes way for demonic deceit and control. A poverty spirit can grip peoples' imagination until they have given up all hope.

Do you know where a poverty mentality is commonly found? *In our churches!* Some churches have elevated poverty next to holiness. This is a blatant lie against God's covenants in the Bible. God is a good God. He wants to bless and save, not curse and destroy. Anyone or anything that substitutes man-made traditions for God's clear word opens the way for something less than God's favor. Lack of true knowledge is destructive of our peace.

You won't find a poverty mentality in the board rooms of Wall Street, or the marketplaces where we shop, or in the manufacturing plants where we work. Why? Because successful businessmen have enough sense to know that their purpose is to make a profit. Bill Gates didn't develop Microsoft Windows just for fun. He did it for profit. Biblically speaking, God is a capitalist. He is for ownership and multi-generational blessings. He wants us to be well-off now and hand off a heritage later.

Poverty Hobbles the Ministry

Profit is not inherently evil. If we don't embrace greed, having abundance is a blessing. Profit is the reward of productivity. Capitalism is not evil. Even a church, which is a non-profit organization by legal definition, must stay in the black or it will soon have to close its doors. A poverty mentality chokes the life out of families and churches. We should love poor people but hate the poverty mentality that haunts them. Obedience to God's word will eventually lift people out of their impoverished culture.

Many pastors have struggled with a spirit of poverty on their church boards and among their members. Maybe the pastor himself is afflicted by an attitude of "there is never enough money." Their spiritual checking account has NSF written all over it. Their faith level is sunk down and needs a lift. You can see a spirit of poverty manifest in the church property. It may look primitive or cheap. Perhaps they don't paint the building or keep it clean. Maybe the restrooms look like a truck stop. Outsiders will take one look and conclude that the church is broke. Who wants to identify with a failing business? Who wants to invest in a losing enterprise? That's a poor testimony for Christ. You can easily see it in the minimum pay scale given to a pastor. He may have to fight all kinds of pressure in his home because he isn't paid a decent living wage.

I remember what it was like when I was a young pastor in my first church. I was working hard to build up the church and to take care of my family. I was living on a barely-get-by salary. Finally, by making sacrifices in my budget, I could afford the first new car I had ever purchased. It was a Plymouth, a demo that a dealer in my church let me have for a very low price. The first Sunday it was parked beside the sanctuary, I overheard a woman in my church saying, "That car is too nice for a preacher to drive."

What made her say something like that? Those words didn't come from God. No, a spirit of poverty from the devil influenced her. Her speech betrayed what was in her heart. That kind of thinking plays right into the devil's hands. Her words hurt me and discouraged me.

I had to learn that God wants me to prosper. I came to believe that it is not unrighteous of the Lord to reward my years of preparation and labor with an honorable salary.

Since then, I have learned a great deal about money and the ministry. One thing I have seen after 40 years of ministry is that most churches don't pay their pastors enough. If they did, more of the children of those pastors would follow them into the ministry. That is usually God's will—that our own sons and daughters might be disciples of the Lord and grow up with a love for God's work.

Christianity is meant to be multi-generational. We should apprentice our own children into the work. The sons and daughters of God's servants are a natural pool from which God can select some to be called into the ministry. Many preacher's kids overcome bad situations. But not all. Some of them deeply resent the way their parents were treated by the church. They want nothing to do with a system that operates with a plantation mentality. Can you blame them?

I remember visiting a parsonage[3] occupied by a fellow pastor across town years ago. He and his wife and two small children lived in a home owned by the church next door. I admired the zeal for God's work this young pastor displayed. But his family was under pressure. When I walked into their house, I had to carefully climb up the broken front porch steps, so I wouldn't stumble. It was dangerous. The wife apologized, saying, "I have been asking the church board to get this fixed for months," she said.

I had another pastor friend whose parsonage had no air conditioning. His wife had become ill from the summer heat. The church was prospering under his leadership, but no one was sensitive to his personal needs. God is not unrighteous to forget the labor of love of his workers, but religious people can be neglectful.

These incidents remind me that pastors today should never live in a parsonage. They miss too many benefits if they do. They need the financial security of personal home ownership. They should be given a tax-free housing allowance (documented in the minutes of the church's annual business meeting) and encouraged to buy their own home. Under current law, ordained ministers can also deduct the interest on their home mortgage when they file their income tax. This is practical, legal, and biblical. This is good stewardship.

---

[3] A parsonage is a residence that a church owns. It is provided for the use of the pastor. Many denominations still use this system.

Let me examine for you some of what the Bible has to say about money, especially as it relates to the work of the ministry. Even so, there is just too much in the Bible on this topic for one brief book to cover it all.

What if I told you that the Bible has over 500 verses about prayer? Would you believe it was important? Of course. What about faith, almost 500 verses as well? There are over 2,000 verses in the Bible that deal with money!

Most of the parables Jesus taught were on money. Money was often the determining factor in the Bible's accounts of how people responded to the kingdom of God. Yet whenever a preacher talks about money, our first reaction is critical: "There he goes again!" We should be thankful for any Bible teacher who dares to elucidate the whole counsel of God's word.

Overcoming Opinions

There is much ignorance and many misguided notions on this subject, plus many vain traditions that confuse the issue. It would be easier to stay silent. Is it worth the effort? Yes, it is. God insists that we teach the whole counsel of his word. Why? Because the Lord wants the well-being of his people to increase.

Therefore, we must learn how to keep the devil away from our stuff and learn how to kick the thief out of the church's storehouse. If we don't, then Christians will stay broke, the work of the church will be hindered, and the wicked people of the world will keep all the wealth. Let's aim a spotlight on the thief in *your* storehouse.

Let me caution you concerning this: once you come to understand a new truth from the Lord, you become responsible for walking in the light of that truth. Ignorance is no longer an excuse.

Ask God to help you grapple with these concepts. Once

understood, they are liberating. In the wrong hands they are injurious. I acknowledge the risk of carnal preachers trying to manipulate God's people with guilt to enrich themselves. Shame on them. But humble servants of truth are welcome.

Humbly, we approach this revelation of God's word. Pray this prayer with me: "Lord, you are worthy of worship and offerings. We submit our opinions to you. Lord. For too long we have been paralyzed by traditions and false notions. Open our minds to remove confusion and fear so we can think clearly and act righteously. We submit to your word. May your work prosper. Show us your ways and bless our lives. Amen."

God's word has defined the blessings that come by his covenants to God's people. "But remember the LORD your God, for it is he who gives you the ability to produce wealth, and so confirms his covenant, which he swore to your forefathers, as it is today" (Deuteronomy 8:18 NIV).

The power to get rich comes from God. The ability to create wealth is included in the covenant blessings of the Bible. God wants some of you reading this book to become millionaires, and thus fulfill your calling!

Yet, the majority of God's people are ignorant of these provisions and therefore don't expect prosperity. A little basic Bible research will show us that we hold many unbiblical beliefs regarding our own money and church finances. Too often, because we mishandle something God calls "sacred," we unwittingly shoot ourselves in the foot when it comes to qualifying for God's blessings.

I know what this is like because of my own experiences. Much of my life as a minister I experienced a cycle of sufficiency and of lack, having extra and then not having enough. I hated this up-and-down cycle. Surely God had promised better things. I certainly believed the Bible. God knows I was sincere.

A Thief in the Storehouse

Do you know what I was doing wrong? I was eating my seed. Every time God would bless me, I would consume it on myself, thinking all his blessings were for *my* benefit. Then, with no seed left over to sow, I would enter another time of leanness. No wonder I was on a financial roller-coaster. I didn't realize that the poverty mentality of the typical small church system had affected my thinking about myself.

Besides my own ignorance, our religious traditions work to impoverish ministers. Most lay people consider a new job offer based on an increase in pay, added benefits, or other factors of promotion that accompany increased responsibilities. But not pastors. They are expected to work purely for eternal rewards. Often pastors are idealistic and somewhat naive about their own compensation. I know I was. They may think that it is unspiritual to negotiate for a better pay package. They may think they have no need of a retirement program. They may not think long-range at all. God wants us to use wisdom.

I had the privilege of being pastor to a wonderful older couple who had returned from decades of service in New Guinea where they had brought the gospel to primitive tribes. They came home successful in their mission but impoverished in their lifestyle. With no retirement, having sold everything and saved nothing, they were dependent on their children for lodging and support. Is this any way to treat valued servants in their golden years?

Walmart clerks have stock options. What do old missionaries have? We need a new paradigm for church finances, one that is based on New Testament apostolic perspectives, not stale religious traditions.

God has a wonderful solution that works for everyone, a simple plan that ensures the prosperity of believers and adequately underwrites his work as well.

The fundamental secret is sowing: sowing to our own

future (saving) and giving away a portion of what is ours. Sowing is something farmers understand. They know that if they don't sow, they will have no crop next season. They must sow consistently. And they can't eat all the seed.

Be Happy and Sow

We must learn to sow during seasons of abundance to ensure a future harvest. I now rejoice when it is my turn to give. Why? Because I know for certain what lies ahead. I know that if I am patient, I will reap. I have begun to tap into God's law of endless supply.

"Now He who supplies seed to the sower and bread for food, will supply and multiply your seed for sowing and increase the harvest of your righteousness; you will be enriched in everything for all liberality, which through us is producing thanksgiving to God" (2 Corinthians 9:10-11).

The seed to sow and the bread to eat both originate from God. I eat the bread and I sow the seed. If I sow, God will supply me with more seed. That's how it works. God created these seasonal cycles.

We must also learn to sow during seasons of leanness. Why? Because what you have in your hand, while it may not be enough to see you through, may be seed that will multiply and become your miracle. When what you have in your hand is not enough to meet your need, you can sow it into good ground and it can become seed. Find your good ground to sow.

Remember the widow who fed Elijah? She didn't have enough, so she sowed into the man of God. Remember the boy's five loaves and two fishes? The boy put his small meal into the hands of Jesus and it fed a multitude. They overcame their fear and gave first to God. They tapped into the law of seedtime and harvest. When we turn loose of our small portion and put it into anointed hands, it gets multiplied and given back, exponentially increased. The widow who fed

Elijah survived the drought. As for the boy with the small meal? I think Jesus gave him the baskets of leftovers!

God has built into creation the power to multiply our resources. Isn't that wonderful? We can recognize this law of sowing and reaping and understand how it operates.

Restoring Financial Integrity

Revival and restoration always brings with it a return to *financial integrity.* Handling other peoples' money or our family budget is a reality check. Did you know Judas was a thief? Jesus put him into position as his ministry team treasurer, right where his corrupt heart would be disclosed. Yet the apostles in Acts were entrusted to receive huge offerings to personally distribute to the poor. Their proven character in this made them worthy of heavenly riches to distribute.

Most of us reading this would never dream of violating our covenant oath to our spouse, would never think of cheating on our marriage partner by having an affair with someone else. Why? Because we would lose our integrity. Most of us would never think of embezzling funds from our employer at work, putting our hand in the till, diverting dedicated funds into our own pocket. Why? Because that would violate our integrity. Most of us would never think about taking the stand in court and lying under oath, swearing falsely. Why? Because that would violate our integrity.

Integrity is exactly what God required of Abraham so the Lord's covenant with him would be fulfilled. God said to him, "walk before me and be blameless (have integrity)." (Genesis 17:1) God made Abraham, Isaac, and Jacob wealthy. When Jacob encountered God, he made a vow, saying, if God will keep me and prosper me, "I will give a tithe to You." (Gen 28:20-22)

Yet many of you reading these words have lost your

integrity. And you've lost it over money. You have gone so deeply into debt that you can't pay your bills on time. You can't keep your promises anymore. A piece of plastic has made you into a liar. You no longer belong to God, you belong to some credit card company. You have forfeited your liberty and become a slave to the lender. You have decided to indulge your desires to the point that you no longer have any wiggle room in your budget. If God said to give or go, you would have to say, "I owe my soul to the company store."

Some of you have made up excuses so that you can dishonor God with your finances. You rob God and assume he understands. You say, "I had a business failure," or "This has been a tough year." Not only do you never tithe—which makes you a thief—but you attempt to deceive God and man by giving offerings and calling it a tithe when you know it isn't. That makes you a liar. You pray harder and yet still feel condemned.

You rob God, you hurt your family's future, you hinder the work of the church, and you live the life of a hypocrite. Because of lack of faith, lack of understanding, or lack of courage, you have lost your financial integrity. If you don't repent and act to correct this, you will never regain it.

View debt as your enemy. This is no time to surrender or compromise. Don't make peace with your enemies. Don't think that living in continual debt is normal or healthy. Don't allow the poverty which gripped your parents or grandparents to grip you. Break out of the generational curse of poverty. Act in faith so that you can pave the way for your children to be blessed. It may take time, but you can do it.

The gospel is good news. Jesus began his public ministry by proclaiming the year of the Lord's favor (Luke 4:19). On God's calendar, this was the Year of Jubilee, the year of God's "Debt Cancellation Program." This was the year slaves were set free, debts were forgiven, and the inheritance went back to its owner. You have arrived in the kingdom at the right time to inherit your blessing. Put your faith in God and *act!*

In Philadelphia, my wife and I walked up in a protected downtown park to view the Liberty Bell, a national symbol. It is inscribed with a portion of this verse from Leviticus 25:10- *"And you shall consecrate the 50th year and proclaim liberty throughout all the land to all its inhabitants. It shall be a Jubilee for you, and each of you shall return to his possession, and each of you shall return to his family."*

The gospel of God's grace has provided an avenue of escape from the curse of poverty. Disorder, divorce, confusion, despair: they are no longer part of your predicted lifestyle. Instead, you can expect mercy and favor. God has proclaimed liberty throughout our land.

Don't Sink with Debt

Personally, and globally, we are drowning in a sea of debt. The world economies are like the great ocean liner, the Titanic, luxurious and arrogant, but ignorant of the impending judgment lying directly in their path. So many of us are busy polishing brass on the Titanic. The builders of the Titanic were certain that she was unsinkable. They didn't provide the lookouts with binoculars. Full-speed ahead on her maiden voyage, they couldn't see the iceberg in time to turn. Why bother? "Even God can't sink the Titanic," the builders had said. The ship sailed at top speed through the night directly into disaster. Arrogance always blinds us to our urgent need to repent.

But it is not too late. You have time to send out an SOS. An SOS is a universal signal calling for help. God's debt cancellation program is just a prayer away. You are one step away from beginning to obey God. Call on God for mercy and act in faith that he will hear you and help you. Send an SOS to heaven.

On the Titanic, the emergency signal SOS meant "Save Our Souls." Your financial SOS stands for three things that will turn your life away from financial disaster—*Sanctify*, *Organize*, and *Sow*. Get off the Titanic of debt and doom. Send out your SOS by following these three simple principles.

SOS #1- Sanctify the Tithe. Acknowledge that the tithe is God's sacred portion. Give it to God and turn it loose, no strings attached. You can't turn it into a designated offering because God has already designated it for his ministry. Begin with the tithe because this cancels the devil's right to rob you. Stop the thief from stealing your bread. When you give God his portion first, it causes a blessing to rest on the remaining 90% in your house. Begin to tithe, begin today, and watch God come to your defense.

SOS #2- Organize your Finances. Use a written budget to order your spending. Stick to it. Pray over it. Put essentials like utilities and groceries at the top of the list, right after the tithe. Yes, put tithes first. If you love God, you can do it. Love God more than Sears or Mastercard. Practice self-denial and forgo luxuries until the important needs are met first. Put your family ahead of your own pleasure. If need be, go on an "entertainment diet."

Here are some other pointers: Always pay your taxes on time. Save your receipts and tax records. Put on paper a list of where the money comes from and where it goes. Know when bills are due so you won't be late. Know how much you have in the bank so you won't bounce checks. Keep a cushion in your checking account and never write it down to zero. Always reconcile your banking statement the same week it arrives in the mail. Limit how much cash you carry on you—it's hard to track. Don't let debit cards deceive you into spending frivolously or impulsively. Maintenance and repair your car. Don't buy a new one; save up for a good used one.

Treat your household like a small business and be businesslike about planning ahead, paying your bills, and paying your taxes. Make it your goal to get out of debt. Dave Ramsey in his book *The Total Money Makeover,* teaches an excellent method: pay off the smallest bill first, then roll over what you save each month to the next largest bill, and so on until you have eliminated all debt.

You and your spouse should agree together to establish some financial goals and pray together about them. Get financial counseling if need be. Make your finances serve your goals of obeying God and blessing your family.

Do your work heartily, as unto the Lord. Be a loyal and productive employee. Take pride in your work. Be on time and don't cheat your boss. Catch a kingdom perspective. It is a privilege to have a job. Be grateful for the skill God gave you. Do your work for the glory of God.

"Whatever you choose as your life work, do it well. Don't be content with sheer mediocrity. Do your job so well that nobody could do it better. Do it so well that all the hosts of heaven and earth will have to say, 'Here lived a man who did his job as if God Almighty called him at this particular moment in history to do it.'" (Dr. Martin Luther King Jr., Ebony Magazine, 1956).

We have a royal bloodline in Christ. As kings and priests, our lives are to be lived for God and the advancement of his kingdom regardless of our vocation. In fact, the kingdom *is* our vocation, even if our paycheck is written by AT&T. All work is noble when done for the glory of God and the benefit of others. As his workers, we are princes and princesses in training to manage his kingdom.

SOS #3- Sow seeds into your future. By this I mean save 10% for the future. Pay God first, pay yourself second, and then pay your bills, in that order. By "pay yourself" I mean save something. You owe it to your family to save a part of every paycheck. Be systematic about saving money, both for short term goals and for retirement. Never spend all your income, but always save part of it to build up a reserve. If you have a cushion in savings, then you won't be tempted to use credit or be driven into debt to meet urgent needs that always come up.

A savings account can protect you from becoming a slave to a credit card. Debt takes the joy out of life. Tithe the first 10%, save the second 10%, and live on the remaining 80%. If you do this consistently, you will always prosper. If you have a savings account, you will always have a cushion, a reserve fund so you can fix problems and handle emergencies. You can also bless the poor, give on special occasions, and fulfill your pledges for worthy projects. Save toward home ownership. Eventually real estate appreciates in value.

God notices our acts of charity. Cornelius, the first Gentile convert, was chosen by God to hear the gospel not only because he prayed, but also because of his alms[4] (Acts 10). He attracted God's favor because of how he generously handled his money.

Be a merciful giver. Don't consume all your seed. Seed for sowing is God's biblical plan for multiplying your resources. Use your faith to expect God to help you have even more seed for sowing. Remember what Jesus said, *"It is more blessed to give than to receive."*

If you take heed to what I am saying, you will be investing in your future. You were created by God and God

---

[4] Alms are personal gifts distributed out of love or mercy. They are private acts of charity. Giving to the poor is one of the three things, which, if done in secret, the Father has promised to publicly reward. (Mt. 6:1-4)

doesn't make junk. You have a hope and a future. Your future has blessings promised to believers, thanks to the grace of our Lord Jesus Christ.

Expect God's goodness. Don't blame God for misfortunes. Keep your faith during trials. Guard your heart. The opposite of hope is despair. Despair is the devil's paint brush, tarnishing everything that is cut off from God. But hope is the oxygen of heaven, pouring joy into everyday life. Obeying God releases hope.

Finding your purpose in life includes your vocation. All work is holy when it is done unto the Lord. Every believer is endowed with some spiritual gift and has a ministry. In the natural, God has given you motivational gifts and talents, which when harnessed by training and diligence, are designed to serve others while blessing you. Knowing your calling will help you adopt the discipline it takes to succeed. I recommend Dr. John Stanko's book, *I Wrote this Book On Purpose So You Can Find Yours!* [5]

Do you know your appointed purpose? Why were you born? Why did God save you? Why here? Why now, today? Discover why God put you on planet earth. Talk with your pastor or your spouse. Seek the Lord by reading the Bible and waiting on him in prayer. God delights to give us wisdom. If you find purpose for living in God, then you will adopt the disciplines needed to be successful. And, you'll be happy! Finding your purpose will help you prosper but your purpose is always about more than just making money.

As Dr. James Dobson says, "I have concluded that the accumulation of wealth, even if I could achieve it, is an insufficient reason for living. When I reach the end of my days, a moment or two from now, I must look backward on something more meaningful than the pursuit of houses and

---

[5] www.purposequest.com

land and machines and stocks and bonds. Nor is fame of any lasting benefit. I will consider my earthly existence to have been wasted unless I can recall a loving family, a consistent investment in the lives of people, and an earnest attempt to serve the God who made me. Nothing else makes much sense."

The restoration of God's redemptive purpose in our lives includes the restoration of financial integrity. Integrity refers to the state of being undivided, being consistent inside and out, not a pretender. In other words, what you see is what you get. Authentic people have integrity.

This biblical wholeness includes inner peace and sufficiency in your financial world. That means getting out of debt. You can't get to where you want to go with an albatross of debt hanging around your neck. God wants to restore you to prosperity even as he restores the Church to its manifest destiny of reflecting the fullness of Christ here, on the earth, now.

God's Economy Scandalizes

If you have read this far in my study, then you may already be offended, perhaps even angry. The truth will set you free—but first it makes you mad!

The word "offended" in the Greek New Testament means to be scandalized, made to stumble. Why? Because God's word seems radical when we first hear it. We stumble when we first run into truth. God's ways and thoughts are higher than ours. Truth always requires repentance, a change of mind. God's truth offends our flesh; our carnal ways and ideas. Truth sounds like heresy if we have never heard it before. Do you have the courage to read on?

We have adopted so many vain traditions regarding money. I've been reluctant to teach about money since I know the enemy will accuse me of being self-serving. Yet the Lord has given me instructions. He told me, *"If you don't teach this, you're not my man."* Sometimes I go to minister God's word in new situations but first state my wish that no collections or honorarium be made for me.

How important is it for a church to get its priorities right about money? The apostles established a great deal of fundamental doctrine for the church regarding finances. If you went through your Bible and cut out all the scriptures regarding money, you've have a gutted Bible, shredded, left in tatters.

For instance, Paul wrote to Timothy about compensating gospel workers. He said the provision for the preacher should come first in the church's budget. *"The hardworking farmer ought to be the first to receive his share of the crops"* (2 Timothy 2:6).

First? Before property or buildings or missions? Yes, first means first. The traditional tendency is to give God's servants the leftovers. I've heard churches say, "We can't afford to pay our preacher that much." They didn't mean they couldn't—they really meant they wouldn't. They had their priorities wrong. This is shameful. God doesn't want the leftovers.

As Malachi said, try giving your governor the sick cow (or in modern terms, a broken-down car). See if he'll put up with it! (Mal. 1:6-8) Where's the honor in that? That's called offering a "lame sacrifice." A lame sacrifice is unworthy. It is something less than your best. God is offended by such offerings and rejects them. But a religious mindset thinks, *"Save the used tea bags for the missionaries."*

Religious traditions can be so strong that they nullify the word of God. We need to be realistic about this fact. We need to understand that when we teach something from the Bible, even if it is Scriptural, it isn't being spoken into a vacuum. Our message is often "over-writing" things already present in our thoughts. Old ways conflict with new truth.

Our previous opinions will resist any newer word coming from God. Many of these old doctrines are not based on the whole counsel of God's word in the Bible but on half-truths. They were formed by habits created by institutions generations ago. Just because our church has always done it that way doesn't make it right. God's way works best, if we are open to consider it and apply it.

Ask yourself these two practical questions. 1) What does the Bible say? 2) Where's the fruit of that method

Anything that prevents repentance or replaces God's word will blind us and deafen us. Anything not of faith is sin. Faith comes from God's word, not from traditions.

Isaiah says that even good religious people can harden their heart and close their ears. Read Isaiah 6:9 which is quoted by Jesus in Matthew 13:14. *"For the heart of this people has become dull..."* Sadly, spiritual deafness is epidemic among modern churches. What is the primary obstacle to God's power? *Man-made traditions!*

Any time we think know something, or think we have everything figured out, we subconsciously close our mind to a new idea. The moment we do this, we stop being a learner. Disciples are learners. We are followers of a person, Jesus, and he is taking us somewhere. If we are not listening, we become impervious to God's word. We substitute our opinions for God's revelation. We backslide and start living by tradition rather than by faith based on God's *proceeding* word.

The Fog of Traditions

In this area of money, our traditions have created many strange situations. Sometimes churches will have an odd way of milking the crowd for offerings, perhaps taking too much time or pressuring people to give. This usually happens because God's word concerning giving has not been taught. Manipulating people to give is always wrong. It trespasses against a person's conscience and leaves them feeling condemned. Giving based on faith or obedience is clean and holy and produces joy.

In some cases, ministers are relegated to preaching while deacons or a church board controls the finances. Biblically, deacons are servants, not governing leaders. This method is out of order. It can neutralize five-fold headship of a pastor or frustrate the grace of apostolic initiative.[6]

Who is properly responsible? Somebody must be in charge or accountable. I'll give some precautions and guidelines at the conclusion of this book.

In the New Testament Church, those called to preach the gospel controlled the flow of church finances. The deacons disbursed it according to the wishes of the apostles.

Apostles are God-called divinely-appointed five-fold ministers (Eph. 4:11). They are authorized to handle the tithes. The elders and deacons were trustworthy helpers chosen by them. They were authorized to handle offerings and distribute charity to the poor. Why is this important? Because—*whoever controls the money controls the church.*

I'm not saying you can't have a qualified board of advisors—godly businessmen included. But I am saying that if carnal men (people not chosen by God, not called, not set apart for the gospel, not anointed to lead) try to control the church's purse strings, they'll choke off the flow of God's blessings.

Listen: *it matters to God who controls the money.* In the Book of Acts, offerings were laid at the apostles' feet, not the

---

[6] Church structure is a topic I address in more detail in my series on Emerging Apostles and the Developing Church.

dseacons (Acts 4:32-5:4). You ask, *"Isn't it unspiritual to be concerned about money?"* Not if spiritual men chosen by God administrate the money; then it becomes holy.

If handling money is unspiritual, then why does Paul's letter to the Corinthians have three times as much to say about money as it does about love? Compare 1 Cor. 13 to 2 Cor. 8-9 and you'll see thirty-nine verses on money and thirteen verses on love. Maybe how we handle money shows how much we really love God. Love can be tracked in a checkbook.

Before John Wesley died, he had set an example of how to handle money in his personal life. He set his budget, lived on it, and gave away everything else to further the gospel. In 1731, he started the practice of giving to the poor. As an educated professor and great preacher, he was one of the richest men of his day. Yet he never lived a life of extravagance. He was a giver.

Some of Wesley's final words to his followers deplored their lack of compassion for the poor and their excessive consumption. He preached that not only should Christians tithe, but they should give away all extra income beyond what their family needed. Wesley believed that as a Christian's income rose, their giving level should rise, *not* their lifestyle. [7]

God's kingdom includes a fiscal policy. Saying "Jesus is Lord" is merely an anemic confession if we exclude money from his rule. Is Jesus the ruler only of immaterial things? Doesn't God's kingdom impact morality, relationships, integrity, and ethics as well as heart motivations? Have you given God permission to address how you handle your money? Have you ever considered the possibility that you

---

[7] Ref: Dr. White, 1988, Christianity Today, from *Int'l Christian History Magazine*, 1921

can love God, go to church, yet commit sin with your money? Obeying God's word protects us from financial sin. The most serious sin regarding money is covetousness, which is a form of idolatry. This is very serious.

Whoever controls the money controls the church

God's ways will work according to well-defined laws. The law of sowing and reaping is a case in point. For instance, under the Old Covenant, Israel had a miraculous provision in the wilderness each morning called manna. But when they entered Canaan, the supply of manna suddenly stopped. They had to begin sowing and reaping to eat in the Promised Land. Yes, they inherited houses and lands and farms they did not build or plant. But blessings for the next generation required that they immediately begin sowing from their bounty. It is foolish to expect God to provide a miracle to get you out of financial trouble, when you stubbornly, habitually, willfully, fail to sow and reap.

The law of sowing and reaping cannot be avoided in the matter of giving. God invites us to tap into his wonderful principle of multiplying our resources by participating in the spread of the gospel. *"Anyone who receives instruction in the word must share all good things with his instructor. Do not be deceived: God cannot be mocked. A man reaps what he sows."* (Galatians 6:6-7)

The question is, who do we sow into? Usually we think in terms of *what* or *where* to sow: which church, what ministry, what non-profit organization. Here, the Lord says it is a person; the instructor he has sent to you; the minister who is giving you spiritual food from God's word. In this case, it was the apostle Paul.

Concerning money, God cannot be deceived. There is an obligation upon all who hear the word to partner with those who deliver it. You cannot make a mockery of God's justice. He keeps the books and he will always see to it that you reap what you sow, just more of it. This law is universal. In this application of Scripture, we are told to sow into the lives of those who teach us God's word.

Giving works when it comes to alms. Alms refers to charity. It is an aspect of giving to the needy. Jesus said in Matthew 19:21, *"If you want to be perfect, go, sell your possessions and give to the poor, and you will have treasure in heaven. Then come, follow me."* Proverbs 22:9 says, *"A generous man will himself be blessed, for he shares his food with the poor."*

Giving to the poor is lending to the Lord. He will repay. The apostles in the New Testament were quick to remember the poor. Jim Elliot, the martyred missionary, famously said, *"He is no fool who gives what he cannot keep, to gain what he cannot lose."*

These laws of sowing and reaping are revealed in Scripture and reflected in nature. They apply to planting and reaping, seedtime and harvest. They work based on definite ways and means. These ways include being diligent in a consistent way, stewarding our resources wisely, investing in good soil so we can expect an abundant return, being liberal instead of stingy, not oppressing the wage earner or defrauding employees, and setting our living standard and sticking to it even when God keeps prospering us. These principles are part of God's laws, evident in nature and laid out for us in his word.

Prosperity comes when we know and practice God's financial covenant. A covenant has an agreement, provisions between two parties. "If you, then I." It isn't like the world's system. Crafty businessmen are mystified by God's methods. The world says, "Get all you can, while you can." God says, "Give it away so you can have more." The world says, "Whoever accumulates the most toys, wins." God says, "A man's soul doesn't consist of the abundance of his possessions."

I believe God is reforming our thinking about money.

Understand, hoarding is a sin. Giving is a blessing. Just as the Scripture says that "the wealth of the wicked is laid up for the righteous," so also the wealth of the righteous is laid up for the poor of the earth, so that they may hear the gospel and be saved. I heard the Spirit of the Lord saying, *"Misery to the miser and surplus to the sower."*

We need the word of God to reprogram our thinking about money. For example, people say money is evil. No, it isn't. The Bible says the *love* of money is evil. It is a heart matter. In the New Testament, the apostles had a great deal to say about financial matters. Let us study their doctrines so we can return to a truly Christian lifestyle in the way we handle money.

God Is Not Stingy

UNDERSTAND, GOD ISN'T CHEAP. Nor is he stingy. He is extravagant. Why, heaven's streets are paved with pure gold. My mother once heard a word from the Lord that admonished her, saying if she didn't appropriate the rich blessings he had freely given, she was like a miser. She was being stingy with herself! God is generous, not stingy. Do you know what a miser is? A miser is somebody who withholds what is due when it is in their power to give it. Don't say, "But I'm not worthy to receive God's blessings." Nonsense. Jesus died on the cross to freely give you his gift of righteousness. He qualified you for blessings!

Proverbs 3:27 says, *"Withhold not good from them to whom it is due, when it is in the power of thine hand to do it."* Remember, "Misery to the miser; surplus to the sower." God certainly has a way with words.

Many religious people are misers. They have no grace to give. They are tightwads. The opposite should be true since gratitude and generosity are signs of God's grace. Sadly, the more religious somebody becomes, often the cheaper they act. My daughter has been a waitress. She tells me that her worst tables were the Sunday church crowds. They often demand extra service but skimp on the tips. Then, after being rude and cheap, they leave a tract. Their stinginess disqualifies their witness.

Religious legalists are always stingy. They can tithe right down to the penny, but begrudge God every cent. God isn't that way at all. In nature, God is known for his abundance. All of creation shows how God fills every available space with life. Have you ever fished in the ocean? The rich variety is amazing. It just teems with life. Our Creator showers us with excess. God always has more than enough. He gives us extra, so we will have some to give away. God is extravagant with his riches of grace.

The nature of Jesus wasn't to hoard things, but to give things away. Remember the five loaves and two fishes? When Jesus gets his hands on anything, he blesses it, multiplies it and freely distributes it. Is that your attitude? Are you a giver? Ask God to give you grace to do it. Being a giver is a lifestyle for people with small incomes as well as the rich. Even the widow's small coin was noticed by Jesus.

Why does God want us to be givers? Because we are his children, and it is a means to a blessing. We should be like our Father in heaven, who is generous and kind. When we give, we co-labor with God, and by this means, we enter his plan so God can make us wealthy.

Becoming wealthy by itself is not a very worthy goal. In fact, that motive alone can be dangerous. An unsanctified heart is easily infected with greed. A successful person may become hardened by pride.

"What causes fights and quarrels among you? Don't they come from your desires that battle within you? You want something but don't get it. You kill and covet, but you cannot have what you want. You quarrel and fight. You do not have, because you do not ask God. When you ask, you do not receive, because you ask with wrong motives, that you may spend what you get on your pleasures" (James 4:1-3 NIV).

God is not interested in pampering our flesh, but rather in extending his kingdom. God's purposes transcend temporary comforts. True wealth doesn't reside in material things, but in the things of eternity and in precious souls. True riches are found in the knowledge of God. Billy Graham has never amassed worldly wealth, but he has sent millions on ahead in the form of saved souls. Mother Teresa had taken a vow of poverty. But in heaven her reward will be greater than Donald Trump's, yet he also has a stewardship. We'll see who has the best mansion in glory.

Let's examine our attitudes toward money. As we do so, realize that our attitude toward giving is simply a barometer of our love relationship with God. *Money in church is like sex in marriage— it isn't everything, but it is important!*

Having a heart to give is not necessary to go to heaven or to have eternal life. It is not as fundamental as justification by faith or water baptism. But it is a marker of growth and trust. Stewardship is the strong meat of righteousness that every developing believer can take in, understand, and obey.

Ritualistic giving has no heart satisfaction, either for God or the giver. "Sacrifice and offering you did not desire, but my ears you have pierced; burnt offering and sin offering you did not require. Then I said, 'Here am I, I have come- it is written about me in the scroll, I desire to do your will, O my God; your law is within my heart.'" (Psalms 40:6-7 NIV)

God desires our heart more than our gifts. If he has our heart, our gifts will follow. Like John Hagee says, "Show me your checkbook and I'll show you what gods you are serving."

A Thief in the Storehouse

Yes, we give solely because God is worthy. Yes, we can also expect blessings to follow. But if not? Then we give out of love anyway. We obey God because he is God. Jesus said, "If you love me, you will keep my words." Love for God will move us to honor him with our offerings.

There is another motivation: doing what is right. It is the right thing to do, that the God who saved us be worshiped with our gifts. Offering up sacrifices is a universal act of worship, even in pagan religions. How much more should we not give offerings to the Living God? Giving is an act of righteousness, borne out of our desire to express gratitude to God who is our gracious Redeemer. Our righteous acts are a testimony that God is worthy of devotion. An altar of sacrifice is right.

Listen: you and I *need* to give. It does something good inside us. Giving is right thing to do. Jesus submitted to the rite of being baptized in water so that he could fulfill all righteousness, not because he needed to repent. Jesus said, *"For I say to you, that unless your righteousness surpasses that of the scribes and Pharisees, you shall not enter the kingdom of heaven."* (Mt. 5:20 NASB)

Giving is something righteous people do. Jesus said our righteousness must exceed that of the Scribes and Pharisees. Being a giver is one result of being right with God. The Pharisees tithed to the penny, but still fell short of knowing and reflecting God's heart. We ought to out-perform their minimum standard.

We honor God and obey his word so that we are righteous and not rebellious, even if we realize no immediate tangible benefit in our lives. Similarly, I've said I would serve Jesus if there were no heaven or no hell, simply because it is the best and happiest way to live. We don't give to get blessed, we give because we are blessed already. We are loved. We are creatures who worship our Creator. We can't withhold from God the worship due him and still be righteous. We owe tangible expressions of worship to God.

Like Mary, we pour out the costly ointment on Jesus' feet, a "waste of worship" (John 11:2), expecting nothing in return. It was not done to make God do something in exchange. As Bible teacher Dudley Hall says, *"The deception that God can be manipulated leads to disillusionment."* [8] That is an understatement.

Money is a Heart Issue

When the early churches were planted by mobile teams, many of those churches partnered with the apostles to support their mission. Their giving was not as important as their heart relationship; it just confirmed it. Without love, nothing works right in God's kingdom.

Paul testified about the churches in Macedonia, "...beyond their ability they gave of their own accord, begging us with much entreaty for the favor of participation in the support of the saints, and this, not as we had expected, but they first gave themselves to the Lord and to us by the will of God." (2 Cor. 8:3-5 NASB)

Partnering with apostles is a means to divine favor, a source of blessing. This local church committed itself to associate with and support an apostolic company. Money follows relationships between pastors or churches and apostles. Churches that give to missionary[9] outreach are always blessed of God.

---

[8] *Incense and Thunder*, by Dudley Hall, Multnomah Press, 1999

[9] The term "missionary" comes from a Latin translation for the biblical term, apostle. Many modern missionaries are not apostles, just pastors in a foreign country for religious purposes. They lack apostolic grace. Jesus deliberately chose this word for his twelve disciples as he trained them and then sent them.

A Thief in the Storehouse

Nothing on earth reveals our heart so much as what we do with our money. Jesus said, *"Where your treasure is, there will your heart be also."* (Luke 12:34) This is an inviolate rule. I have often tried to prove Jesus wrong about this but never succeeded. I have tried to trust people who were unfaithful with their money, who didn't tithe, who gave only sporadically, or who abused their credit. It always backfired. I have finally realized Jesus is smarter than I am.

Jesus knows people's hearts. Thoughts beget deeds and attitudes control actions. What we do with our money proves where our affections really lie. Spending uncovers our motives. Often, our heart is wrapped up in possessions rather than in God. This becomes idolatry. Covetousness—or greed—is a sign of secret idolatry. Americans may not bow down to man-made idols, but we display major symptoms of idolatry due to jealousy or greed.

We forget that one of the Ten Commandments is *"You shall not covet"* (Deuteronomy 5:21). To covet means to lust after something that is not ours. Lust is invisible to human eyes. You can be a respected businessman in a nice suit serving as a church treasurer and be guilty of the sin of coveting.

Do you remember the story in the Bible where Jesus braided a whip and drove money-changers out of the Temple? I recall when the Lord used this story to ask me a surprising question. *"Would you rather be in the company of Jesus, eating and drinking with sinners, or sitting at the table with the money-changers in the Temple?"* The key phrase was, "in the company of Jesus." My answer was, "Lord, I need a job and the church will pay me." Looking back, I gave the wrong answer and made the wrong decision.

The money-changers were respectable, in a dignified place, selling small animals for travelers to use as sacrificial offerings. They were cleaned up, looking good, and serving God. They made money from religion. Religion is a big business. Jesus didn't go where the money was. He went where the people were who needed him.

Sinners are not like the money changers in the Temple. They are not cleaned up. Their language is not respectable. Their vices can be offensive. They are not religious. In fact, they regularly *sin*. That's why they need a Savior.

What was the outcome of Jesus' interactions with these differing groups of people? The group in the Temple got publicly thrashed, shamed, and expelled. The sinners outside in the streets heard Jesus gladly, interacted with Him freely, and many were saved. Jesus said that his Father's house is a house of prayer. If people in the house would pray, then people in the streets would be saved and know the Lord.

Coveting is a Crime

Covetousness is lust. It is evil. The ironic thing is, even poor people can be guilty of covetousness. You don't need to display wealth to be guilty of this sin. In fact, many wealthy people have open hands and generous hearts, while some poor people are envious of the wealthy. Covetousness may be manifested as an inordinate love for money. This is greed. It always makes the object of its desire into an idol, a false god.

Covetousness can infect corporate groups or leadership teams. Sometimes church boards glance over at the tithe income and start coveting control of God's money. They get their priorities confused. They start dreaming of building monuments to their ambition and forget the admonition, *"You shall not muzzle the ox while he is threshing out the grain."*

Let's not be naive about attitudes regarding the major church revenue stream, the tithe. Grasping after control of a sacred source can be a serious sin. This is "institutional envy." *"Then he said to them, 'Watch out! Be on your guard against all kinds of greed; a man's life does not consist in the abundance of his possessions'"* (Luke 12:15 NIV).

It might be unthinkable as Christians to covet our neighbor's wife, but we may try to covet the tithe. How do we do that? By withholding the tithe or subverting it for some illegal use. We would never think of "cooking the books" if we worked for IBM, but church boards may misappropriate the money intended for those preaching the gospel. If we will repent, God will show us the pathway to righteous prosperity.

The love of money always crowds out the love of God. Jesus said, *"You cannot serve God and money."* He didn't say, "You can try harder and maybe do it," He said, *"You cannot."*

We cannot allow money to become our lord and master. God wants to prosper us, but he doesn't want prosperity to destroy us. Love for God must take priority over love for things, or love for people, or love for power. There is a real danger, that in being blessed, we will honor the gift more than the Giver. Our carnal nature, if left undisciplined, is unable to handle blessings without falling into sin. The discipline of the Christian life—being subject to God's word—protect us from abusing or losing God's blessings.

One Christian discipline is paying the tithe; another is giving offerings. I will say more about the distinction between these two types of offerings later. If we lay our lives down before God and are faithful to him, then he will entrust us with true riches like a master entrusts his chief steward with resources.

God doesn't hesitate to bless those who serve him. A sanctified soul can possess money without money possessing him. One way you can tell if money is possessing you is by your willingness to walk away from it. Can you lay your blessings on the altar?

God blessed Abraham, the father of all who believe.

Abraham was God's friend. He was the father of the Jewish race. He represents faith. Abraham was able to lay the promise, his son Isaac, on the altar. As a result, God made Abraham wealthy and gave him innumerable offspring who produced Israel.

Have God as a Friend

GOD MADE COVENANT promises to Abraham and vindicated him in his trials (Genesis 20:14). Abraham is called a friend of God. This tells us that God wants his friends to do well. Included in the deal God gave to Abraham were material blessings, financial rewards, a permanent heritage of land, a lineage, divine favor, and prosperity. The man of faith, Abraham, inherited God's blessings in a tangible way.

God's people living according to God's word should expect sufficiency to the point of abundance.

Later, God's law given by Moses revealed both blessings and curses concerning money (Deuteronomy 28). Moses represents the Law. The law of God shows that when material wealth is used to worship God, then God will prosper his people. Whether you consider God's blessings from faith or from law, both approaches include provisions for prosperity. In fact, the very nature of blessings includes the idea of increased material well-being.

In the New Testament, both faith and law are realized and fulfilled in Christ. Christ represents grace. Under grace, we have a better covenant, richer blessings, and better promises. God's grace makes us rich. *For you know the grace of our Lord Jesus Christ, that though he was rich, yet for your sakes he became poor, so that you through his poverty might become rich.* (2 Cor. 8:9 NIV).

Any way you look at it—through faith, through law, or through grace—we are King's Kids with a fabulous inheritance. In fact, it is hard to avoid God's blessings.

God's people living according to God's word should expect sufficiency to the point of abundance. You can't help it. His goodness, mercy, and blessings will overtake you. David, an Old Testament prototype of kingdom living, said, *"I would have despaired unless I had believed to see the goodness of the Lord in the land of the living"* (Psalms 27:13). To me, this describes abundance. Abundance means having more than enough.

Do you have more than enough, or do you barely get by? Are you living from paycheck to paycheck? Do you "rob Peter to pay Paul?" Maybe you're living beneath your privileges as a child of God. The age of grace we're in means we have better covenants and better promises than either Abraham or Moses.

God has a provided a way for us to participate in his economic system. This program involves certain covenants God has made (which we must know and understand), certain values he wants us to adopt (such as godliness, stewardship, investment, and liberality), and certain disciplines he wants us to practice (such as praying, tithing, giving, saving, and investing). These *covenants, values,* and *disciplines* all combine to create a lifestyle of freedom from greed, excellence in our labor, and generosity in our giving. *They are the basis for our blessings.*

Many good books have been written by Christian authors on the topic of biblical stewardship, for example, by

Larry Burkett or Dave Ramsey. Most begin with the presupposition that you know and believe the Bible. This is basic to success. You must know God's word if you want to have wisdom. *"My people are destroyed for lack of knowledge."* (Hosea 4:6 KJV).

Next, get your priorities in life lined up right. How do we do that? Love and honor God first; your family second; and your work, third. If your main motivation in life is making more money, then you're mixed up in your priorities. Put worshiping and serving God first. Put your family second. Then, practice wise administration of your own financial realm. Have a godly plan born out of a heart of love.

In God's kingdom, faith works by love. You can't "work the system" and think you can push the right buttons with God. He knows our hearts. Genuine repentance allows us to develop a trusting heart. A heart that is right with God will want to be right with your family and your church. Wisdom, righteousness and liberality are essential elements to biblical prosperity and peace. Get right with God and get right with your fellow man.

Heed this warning: If you don't love righteousness; if you are stewing in bitter envy; if you constantly criticize and complain; if you covet or envy or try to control others; you may as well settle it now—poverty will wrap itself around you like a well-fitting suit.

"He also loved cursing, so it came to him; And he did not delight in blessing, so it was far from him. But he clothed himself with cursing as with his garment, And it entered into his body like water, And like oil into his bones." (Psalms 109:17-18 NASB).

Cursing others always bounces back on you, while a generous soul gets watered by God. God's blessings begin with having a transformed heart that loves to give freely and to forgive quickly.

Your family is a small business. It is an economic administration, a particular kind of unit in God's kingdom. Kingdom principles applied from the Bible will make your home or your business prosper. For example: be a diligent worker, pay God first, pay your taxes second, save a portion for emergencies, plan for retirement, pay your bills on time, don't defraud your employees, invest for increase, plan ahead based on wise counsel, and pass along an inheritance to your children. These are all biblical mandates. They are the essence of stewardship and good administration. Your plan becomes a godly plan when you submit it to the Bible's principles and when you pray over it sincerely.

God's economic system transcends all earthly systems. We are not dependent on the Dow Jones Industrial Averages for our long-term welfare. God blessed Israel during their captivity even while he was judging Egypt. God can feed his children even during times of famine. If you honor God and believe his prophets, you will be established and blessed. God's law of sowing and reaping overrules any economic cycle of growth and recession.

Defining the Tithe

In applying God's laws of economics be sure and practice "first things first." That includes an understanding that God created you and called you and has equipped you for a certain kind of work or vocation. Honest work is good. Laziness is wicked.

Ask God to show you why he placed you on this earth. Find it and get educated and trained to do it. Love your work, pray over it, be dedicated and faithful in it. You were put on this earth to solve other peoples' problems and those people will pay you well when you serve them with your talent and skill. Your labor will bring a financial reward. When that reward comes, you need to find out what God's word says about how to handle your money.

Move up in stages toward prosperity, from working for your money, to saving and investing your money, to having your money work for you. To learn more about this principle, I suggest you read the excellent book, *Rich Dad, Poor Dad*, by Robert Kiyosaki.

Assuming you believe in and practice the Judeo-Christian (or Puritan Principle) of the western work ethic, the next fundamental discipline which is the beginning of obedience to God in financial matters is the practice of tithing.

In the Bible, the word "tithe" means one-tenth. It appears in both the Old and New Covenants. It is a systematic method of returning to God the first ten percent of everything God has given to us. It is not equal giving, but equal sacrifice, proportional to our prosperity. It is not a gift we give, but a debt we pay. We owe God the tithe because he claims it for his use.

"Tithe" means One-Tenth

The tithe occupied a very large part of the Jewish understanding of worship. In Jesus' day, his followers practiced tithing. Paying tithes was assumed, much as paying taxes. It was the cultural norm into which Jesus and the apostles spoke. They presumed their listeners were already tithing as a religious observance.

The New Testament norm was that people gave at least ten percent of their income to God. Why? Because most of the first Christians were Jewish believers. The Jews followed Abraham and the law of Moses. They supported the Levitical pattern of worshiping God with tithes and offerings. Remember, Jesus was a Jew. He grew up in a family that kept the law. In his ministry, he practiced what he preached.

We need to ask ourselves, What's the big deal? Why

does the Bible teach people to tithe?

God has chosen this seemingly mundane activity and has made it into an act of faith and obedience. Giving is really a form of worship. Bringing an offering to the Lord was the fundamental act of honoring God in the Old Testament. *"And none shall appear before Me empty-handed."* (Exodus 34:20 NASB). Under the Law, you did not fulfill worship unless you brought something to sacrifice to God.

In modern Christianity, we have so abandoned our Hebrew roots that we now think singing songs is the fundamental act of worship. Yes, worship in the Spirit must include the fruit of our lips, giving thanks to his name. But, words are cheap. They cost us nothing. Our words are separated from our deeds. We think we can worship with lip-service, but our hearts may be far away from the Lord.

We have divorced Christianity from our patriarchal Hebrew heritage. This is wrong. Doing things that are feeling-oriented cannot be divorced from acts of obedience. There is faith formed first in our heart, then there is faith worked out in our obedience. Spirituality cannot be divorced from reality. Jesus taught action-oriented religion when he called for alms, praying, and fasting (Mt. 6).

Another reason for the importance of the tithe is that it provided the basis for the support of the gospel ministry. It finances the agents of the kingdom. The early New Testament era saw Jewish believers paying tithes to the temple and giving offerings to the apostles—large offerings from property sales. Later, the church became more Gentile in its composition. A transition occurred. The Pharisees and Sadducees and the priestly system rejected the new Christians.

When the temple in Jerusalem was destroyed in 70 A.D,, no funds went to religious buildings any longer but instead went to support the apostles or went to help the poor. This pattern continued until the Roman Emperor Constantine's conversion in the third century and the return of temple worship to Christianity. For its first three centuries the church moved in great apostolic power then it became formalized, institutionalized, and anemic. House churches in the city diminished and facility-based gatherings commenced. We haven't yet fully recovered.

Honoring God with our wealth didn't quit when the Jewish temple worship ceased. Instead, the offerings went into the "new" temple, the Body of Christ, and supported its leaders.

The apostles raised offerings to help poor saints during persecution or famine. The Book of Acts shows that the apostolic church had grace for extraordinary giving. They didn't depend on the government for their safety net. Their giving went well beyond the tithe. The tithe is simply the least we can do. If all you do is tithe, you are a substandard Christian, by New Testament standards.

The preaching of the kingdom of God in the New Testament produced a community of believers who lived sacrificially and honored God financially. The needy among them were helped. The church was a kingdom colony that invoked a blessing from heaven on their surrounding secular community. Coincidental with the advance of Christianity is what missiologists call the "gospel lift." God's advancing kingdom lifts people out of poverty and promotes economic welfare. Citizens under the Lordship of Jesus benefit from his rule. The habitations of darkness who worship idols remain in abject poverty, while by and large, wherever the gospel is obeyed, believed, and received among believers, poverty abates.

The gospel creates an alternative society, a heavenly order. Every government has a tax and God's kingdom is no exception. One way of viewing the tithe is as a "heavenly tax." It supports God's government as administered through his five-fold headship ministry offices. It is a seal that your finances are under God's oversight. It is a systematic investment in heaven. When we give to the gospel's spread, we help to empty hell and populate heaven.

Tithes vs Offerings

THERE IS A DIFFERENCE between tithes and offerings although both are acts of worship. You pay tithes, you give offerings—an important distinction. Biblically, you can't make a freewill pledge or offering until you have first paid your tithes. Otherwise, you will still be robbing God. This often happens based on a common misunderstanding.

Offerings are free-well gifts beyond the tithe. Tithes are an obligation that comes before offerings. Christians can make a $10 donation or a $100 pledge and due to lack of sound teaching, call it a tithe. It is not a true gift or offering until it exceeds ten percent of our income. It is a mistake or a misrepresentation to call an offering a tithe. You may make an offering for any good reason or purpose. But the tithe has a unique place.

The Bible makes a distinction among various kinds of offerings. The tithe is in a class all by itself. The tithe is called "holy unto the Lord." It is sacred. This is not said of any other types of offerings. Tithes are not pledges. Nor are they free-will contributions.

The Bible teaches us that tithes are an obligation we owe to God. After all, our prosperity comes from the riches our Creator placed on or within the earth and the talents or abilities and opportunities he gave to us. Therefore, tithes are a debt that every person owes to God.

Why is this so? Because God has said that the tithe is *holy* and that it is *his*. It doesn't belong to us. He has claimed it as his own, like rent to a landlord. We have no right to keep it. Therefore, we can't give the tithe to United Way or send it to a different place or person at a whim. It isn't ours to decide. We have to do with it what God wants done with it or we are being disobedient.

The tithe is also called a "sacred portion." Sacred means holy, or sanctified. Something that is sacred is devoted to a holy purpose or person. It is set apart from ordinary use.

The tithe is ten percent of the gross of your earnings. The tithe is a percentage of your income. That means that if your income for a year was $45,000, then your tithes for that year are $4,500. That 10% taken off the top of your income shows that you are trusting God's intention to bless you.

If we withhold paying our tithe, it is like we are embezzling funds or defrauding workers. Tithes don't belong to us. They belong to God, and are assigned a specific use, for his priests: leaders who have sacrificed a career or vocation to serve him.

Tithes are also in the category called, "first-fruits." This means they are claimed by God right off the top. Tithes cannot be pushed down to the bottom of the list and given as leftovers. If it is not given first, if it is not the best we have to give, then it is not worthy of the God we worship. Two words always describe tithes: *first*, and *best*.

God is worthy of the first and the best. If it doesn't go to God first, then it lacks the honor it should reflect toward God. Look at what God did to Cain's offering: *"In the course of time Cain brought some of the fruits of the soil as an offering to the LORD. But Abel brought fat portions from some of the firstborn of his flock. The LORD looked with favor on Abel and his offering, but on Cain and his offering he did not look with favor."* (Genesis 4:3-5 NIV).

Abel brought the first-fruits, but Cain brought his gift when he got around to it, "in the course of time." That's why God rejected it. Tithes are in the category of first-fruits. We need to keep first things first.

Likewise, tithes ought to be the best gifts we have. Substandard offerings can't be given as tithes without dishonoring God. (Malachi 1:6-14) Your best offering may not be as valuable as someone else's, but it has to be the best you have.

Offerings are not tithes. They are gifts we freely choose to offer *in addition* to our tithes. Offerings are not obligatory. They flow out of seeing a need or wanting to show love. Offerings are seed for sowing, so we can reap a harvest.

Good stewardship will enable us to have extra, so we can give offerings beyond our tithes. If we can't afford offerings, if we don't have tithing as a regular part of our budget, then we have already lost control of our finances. Anyone who tithes is set on a road toward prosperity. Anyone who gives offerings above the tithe has learned how to multiply their seed and increase their harvest.

Based on over four decades of pastoral experience, I can predict that people who never tithe nor give offerings are headed for financial trouble. Failure to tithe is letting the tail wag the dog. It means you are not ruling over your money. Such issues diminish your inheritance.

Who is Lord over your finances? Does your money act like it's the boss? Does your money rule you, or do you tell it what to do? Does money dictate the will of God to you? The fact is, *money must be ruled over*. Make your money submit to God's will.

Take authority over your budget. Manage it. Have a plan on paper to guide your financial decisions. Begin by tithing. *Honor God first* ahead of all others. This places the Lord's name over your finances. Tithing cancels Satan's illegal claim on your money and puts your money under God's rule. That is good news!

Tithing is an ancient spiritual practice discovered long before the law of Moses. People like Abraham, God's friend, found they could walk in God's favor by honoring him from their wealth. Abraham tithed 10% to God. The Holy Spirit showed him this principle of faith before the Law was written. By setting a pre-selected percentage, God helps us to be consistent in our contributions. Tithing is an act of faith based on knowing God's covenant.

Jesus is a Priest Forever

How well do you know your Bible? Do you appreciate the importance of father Abraham? Abraham is the father of faith (Romans 4:16). He is held up as an example for the New Testament believer (Galatians 3:7). We are to imitate his faith (Hebrews 11:6). We want to walk in his steps of faith, don't we? If so, then we'll have to handle money like he did.

Abraham tithed to a man who blessed him hundreds of years before the Law was given. He had a revelation of how to relate to God financially. His faith affected his giving. How did he do this? After he achieved a great victory in battle and rescued Lot, he tithed to a unique man named Melchizedek, a priest who blessed him. Melchizedek was a type of Jesus.

"And Melchizedek king of Salem brought out bread and wine; now he was a priest of God Most High. And he blessed him and said, 'Blessed be Abram of God Most High, Possessor of heaven and earth; and blessed be God most High who has delivered your enemies into your hand.' And he gave him a tenth of all." (Genesis 14:18-20 NASB).

Psalms 110:4 and Hebrews 7:17 says of Jesus, "Thou art a priest forever after the order of Melchizedek."

Who was this man to whom the father of all believers paid tribute? His name means "king of righteousness." He ruled as king over Salem. Salem means "peace." He was the King of Righteousness, the Prince of Peace, and he ministered symbols of the New Covenant (bread, wine, a blessing) to the prototype believer. Melchizedek was a type of, if not in fact an actual appearance of, the Lord Jesus Christ.

Notice, Jesus is the priest of an eternal order, and he still *receives* (continuous tense) tithes from believers. (Hebrews 7:1-8) For those who object to the pattern of Jewish worship with offerings being given to Levitical priests, I say, it is the biblical pattern. Plus, what about Jesus' priesthood? It is of a different order. It still exists.

Jesus said in John 8:56, *"Your father Abraham rejoiced to see my day..."* When did Abraham see Jesus? Perhaps it was this *christophany*, an Old Testament appearance of the Son of God. God had given Abraham a promise to prosper him (Genesis 12) but that prosperity did not begin until *after* he believed God. Nor did it begin until *after* he had tithed to the Lord.

Christ came to Abraham in the form of Melchizedek and gave him the opportunity to act in faith, to give a tenth of his wealth to the One who interceded for him and was blessing him with the provisions of the promise. He began the cycle of receiving blessings from God. He sowed, then he reaped. When we tithe today, we do it as unto the Lord Jesus Christ. It is personal, based on being chosen, not just a religious exercise.

Jesus has proven to us that he is trustworthy. We honor him out of our material wealth because he has blessed us and given us victory over our enemies. Our faith in Jesus is not misplaced.

Melchizedek extended covenant blessings to Abraham (an interceding priest, the bread and wine, the acknowledgment of God as Provider, and pronouncement of covenant blessings). Abraham, the model of biblical faith, extended covenant response by honoring the Lord by tithing. He didn't have the law and he didn't have religious traditions. He had a revelation that tithing ratified the covenant. Tithing is the fruit of faith in God. It predates the law of Moses.

A Covenant of Blessing

TITHING IS NOT LEGALISM, but honor toward God who is our Creator and Redeemer. It is exercising faith to obtain favor in financial matters. It is a covenant made by God with man. Tithing is an expression of covenant relationship with God. Like all covenants, it has definite "if-then" conditions. Tithing is not as important as repentance, faith, worship, knowing God's word, confessing "Jesus is Lord," or receiving God's spiritual gifts. Failing to tithe won't send you to hell nor will practicing it earn your way to heaven. But it is the fruit a relationship with God expressed in a financial way. Tithing, along with giving to the poor, is a key to achieving stable prosperity in God.

In Genesis 28:20-22, the second mention of tithing occurs in the Bible. It is referenced again in the context of a covenant, with "if-then" conditions:

"Then Jacob made a vow, saying, 'If God will be with me and will watch over me on this journey I am taking and will give me food to eat and clothes to wear so that I return safely to my father's house, then the LORD will be my God and this stone that I have set up as a pillar will be God's house, and of all that you give me I will give you a tenth.'" (Gen. 28:20-22 NIV)

In the context of covenant, God responds to our obedience when we meet the conditions. God has obligated himself to his word and invites us to prove its validity.

The prophet Malachi said, "Bring the whole tithe into the storehouse, that there may be food in my house. Test me in this, says the LORD Almighty, and see if I will not throw open the floodgates of heaven and pour out so much blessing that you will not have room enough for it." (Malachi 3:10)

Do you see the "if-then" conditions? If we bring in the whole tithe, then God will respond with abundant blessings. Notice, Malachi said "the whole tithe," not just part of it. A partial tithe isn't a tithe at all.

Tithing is basically a matter of trusting God. It also requires creating new habits. We ought to learn a new pattern of personal obedience as a lifestyle. This may not be easy at first, especially if we are already in trouble financially. But if you don't start now, when will you?

I began tithing years ago. I have a track record of faithfulness with God. I can testify that he has a history of faithfulness with me. Every time I get a paycheck, every time I receive an honorarium for preaching, I sit down and deduct ten percent for God.

How do you calculate the tithe? I just move the decimal over one place to the left, and I've got it figured out. I do this right away, as soon as I have deposited the check. That way, I establish a habit of faithfulness. I don't want to forget and fail to pay God that which is his. Sometimes people think, "I pay the preacher with my tithe. If I'm not there for church to hear his sermon, then I don't owe anything." That's not true. The tithe is God's. If you NEVER go to church, you still owe it to God.

How would you feel if your employer stuck your paycheck in his wallet and carried it around for two weeks, forgetting to hand it to you? Likewise, we should quickly "remove the sacred portion from our house."

We can take matters into our own hands and change our financial destiny. We don't have to be a victim of circumstances. We don't have to depend on so-called luck. We can cancel curses that have plagued our families for generations. We have power to alter our lives for the better. We can change our future based on how we respond to God's word about money.

How do you decide where or to whom you pay your tithes? In the New Testament, the apostles did not have non-profit corporations. Things were simpler then. The early church gave to a trusted person in the name of the Lord, mainly apostles.

Today we have religious corporations, tax-exempt church status, checking accounts, and computerized debit cards. We also have a lot of people deeply in debt. But God's ways based on God's word will work in any age and in any culture.

The tithe is a universal principle that works with any medium of exchange. If you've got money, then tithe with money. If all you have is chickens and corn, then tithe your produce. If pastors and churches can use laws to set up non-profit organizations and receive contributions via checking accounts, that is well and good. But if you can't, then tithe to the ministry or to the man/woman of God and support the work of the gospel. This is what Christians do in nations which don't allow charitable tax deductions.

Why should the IRS determine whether we will obey God? The laborer is worthy of his hire whether we get a tax deduction or not. God's law is higher than any earthly government. If the tithe isn't meant to support the preaching of God's word, then what good is it? I'm saying this: God is to be honored whether or not we get a tax deduction for it. We give to honor God, not to reduce our taxes. That is a side benefit in America. We can take advantage of it if we are legally able.

The Concept of Holy Things

Holy means "to be consecrated." In a sense, my wife is holy unto me. No other man is entitled to touch her but me, her husband. She and I are sanctified, set apart for each other, to the exclusion of all others.

In the same way, the tithe is holy unto the Lord. It is devoted to God alone. The word ***devoted*** is translated "dedicated" in the King James Version. It is the Old Testament Hebrew word *cherem* (khay'-rem), and is defined in Strong's concordance as "a doomed object; (abstr. extermination), a cursed thing, a dedicated thing, things which should have been utterly destroyed, appointed to utter destruction, something under the ban."

The essential thing about the tithe is that it is destined to be destroyed, annihilated, not stored up, but consumed. In the Old Testament, the priests consumed the tithes and offerings for their food or they burned them entirely by fire on the altar.

In the Bible, devoted things were set apart to God. They were under the ban. God had the right to consume them. God appointed them for destruction.

Here is an amazing fact— God will track down and consume what is his, wherever he finds it. If you keep a devoted thing in your stuff, your stuff gets consumed, *and* you become cursed, since *"...you, like it, will be set apart for destruction."* (Dt. 7:26 NIV). However, if you take the devoted thing out of your house and give it to God, it brings a blessing on your house. You can't keep it, you can't conceal it, and you can't store it up without it bringing a curse on your house. This is a serious issue, isn't it?

The Jericho Issue

DO WE HAVE PERMISSION to take the land? The greatest prayer movement in human history is underway. The most amazing reformation of church leadership ever seen is occurring. There are enemies in the land. Do we have permission to advance and take the land? Will the gospel win? Will we see God's kingdom established in the lives of redeemed humanity?

The crisis of obedience regarding Jericho must be settled. Until Jericho fell, Israel could not take the land. What was the Jericho issue? Who owns the holy portion God claims as his own? God demanded the first fruits of conquest or they would not have authorization to take the rest of the land.

Power by itself cannot defeat the enemy. We need permission, divine authorization, to possess the land.

Spiritually, the church is maturing, developing, and in a sense, it is entering into its Canaan. When we were first saved, we left the bondage of Egypt. We quit wandering in the wilderness and started to possess our inheritance. The good news is, we have crossed into our promised land of salvation. The bad news is, the manna has ceased. Now our supply comes *after* we have sown, not before. We are now dependent on sowing and reaping for our supply. We need to learn this lesson. We're in a new season in God with new laws of prosperity. Obedience to God gives us the right to conquer the land.

When Jericho fell, some items were under the ban (*cherem*), things devoted to God, set apart for the Lord. God told Israel as they prepared to pull down the stronghold of Jericho, *"But keep away from the devoted things, so that you will not bring about your own destruction by taking any of them..."* (Joshua 6:18 NIV). The NASB translation completes this verse, *"so you would make the whole camp of Israel accursed and bring trouble on it."* Here, the many could be affected by the few.

Achan did this very thing (see Judges 7). He stole, and he lied. He took something under the ban. One person's sin endangered the whole nation. He brought a curse on the whole community. When we are in covenant, we affect those around us. God deals with us as a group, not just as individuals. In the same way, a whole church can be held back spiritually by the failure of its members or leaders to respect the tithe. How can this be possible? To understand it, we need to know how God feels about things he has designated as holy.

The phrase "under the ban" appears 13 times in ten verses in the Old Testament in the New American Standard translation. In the King James Version, it is translated as "cursed thing." In the New International Version, it is either "set apart for destruction" or "devoted thing." All these translations are from the same Hebrew word, *CHEREM*.

This Hebrew word is prominent is the story of the conquest of the Promised Land. For instance, it is used in Joshua 6:17-19, 7:1, and 7:11-12. Joshua knew exactly what *cherem* meant because he had been taught its meaning by his mentor, Moses. Anything *cherem* was to be handled with reverence. It was dangerous for anyone not authorized to touch it.

Moses had used this same word in Leviticus 27:28-30 and in Numbers 18:12-14. Joshua knew these words by heart (Joshua 1:7-8). If you read these passages and list the meanings which come out of the text, these truths are evident:

- anything under the ban is holy to the Lord.
- the tithe is holy to the Lord.
- it represents the best we have to offer.
- it represents the first of our increase.
- it must be given to the priests of the Lord.

In addition to these ideas, we see that God intended this principle to never change. Numbers 18:19, 24, and 26 shows us that the tithe for the priests is:

- a perpetual covenant.
- an inheritance to those in the ministry.
- the priests were to tithe off the tithe.

This principle shows us another of the ways in which the Christian community can be rendered powerless before her enemies—by misappropriating things under the ban.

Honoring God's word, praying fervently, maintaining unity, all are essential for spiritual power. What about *handling money righteously?* Israel was defeated before her enemies when they violated this order (Joshua 7:1).

Recovering Reverence

Holy, in the Old Testament, is the Hebrew word, *qodesh* (ko'-desh), defined by Strong's as "a sacred place or thing;

(rarely abstract) sanctity, consecrated, dedicated, hallowed, holiness, most holy, holy day, holy portion, holy thing, saint, sanctuary." When something is holy, God insists it be handled in a prescribed way. This would mean the difference between life and death.

God insists that we reverence him. He is holy and those things he designates as holy must be treated with respect, even his holy prophets who carry his anointing. *"Touch not My anointed, and do My prophets no harm."* (1 Chron. 16.22)

This is true regarding offerings and God's servants. Aaron was appointed by God as high priest. He was anointed by God for his sacred duty. His four sons were named as helpers. Two of them, Nadab and Abihu, acted presumptuously and sinned. They offered unauthorized fire on God's altar (Lev. 10:1-3). Fire came out from God's presence and they were killed. *Moses then said to Aaron, "This is what the LORD spoke of when he said: 'Among those who approach me I will show myself holy; in the sight of all the people I will be honored.'"* (Lev 10:3 NIV)

Remember Uzzah and the Ark of the Covenant? He mishandled the ark and it cost him his life (2 Samuel 6:7). He mishandled something holy, something prohibited, something only the Levites were permitted to handle.

This experience frightened King David. For a while David was afraid to finish bringing the Ark up to Jerusalem. Later, he searched out the prescribed way and completed the Ark's return. Notice, God did not apologize to David for making him feel bad nor did he raise Uzzah back from the dead.

We can't bring holy things down to the level of humanity without judgment breaking out. Likewise, only those set apart by God could handle the tithe. Mishandling the tithe is like touching God's anointed. It always results in spiritual death in the church.

This was demonstrated so plainly in the New Testament, at the beginning of the apostolic community's development. A revival of liberal giving had broken out in the church. Great grace was upon them all. It was accompanied by supernatural miracles.

In the middle of this manifestation of God's glory, Ananias and Saphira conspired to misrepresent their offering (Acts 5). They lied, not to man, but to the Holy Spirit. Under instant judgment from God, both died at the feet of the apostle Peter. Fear came on the whole church. This revival of the fear of the Lord was followed by a great harvest of souls and many miracles. The fear of God precedes revival.

God is holy. He is not like us. He is to be feared. His glory requires that we approach him properly. If we walk in ignorance, God will overlook it for a while. But when we have the light on any truth, when we grow up in God, he requires us to walk in the light. If we turn away from the light, we backslide.

If we are taught the word of God and receive it, we can advance wisely. We can make adjustments to our thinking and our ways. There is no substitute for repentance and obedience.

To paraphrase a quote from Derek Prince, "There comes a time in our walk with God when we can halt all forward progress if we don't hear and obey God's word." He also said, "All progress in the Christian life is by faith."

How we handle money is one of those critical issues. We can decide if we want to go on in God. We can affect our family's destiny, our church's destiny, and even our nation's destiny. We get to choose whether we ride in the Lord's boat or not. The boat with Jesus in it gets the miraculous catch of fish and gets protected from the storm.

Too often we reduce giving to an impersonal act, to a

religious exercise. We remove the priest, the pastor, or the apostle from the picture. No one cares for our soul and no one knows if we're tithing. Is this biblical?

Jesus watched the widow donate her coins. This was a deliberate act on his part. "Jesus sat down opposite the place where the offerings were put and watched the crowd putting their money into the temple treasury. Many rich people threw in large amounts. But a poor widow came and put in two very small copper coins, worth only a fraction of a penny. Calling his disciples to him, Jesus said, 'I tell you the truth, this poor widow has put more into the treasury than all the others.'" Mark 12:41-43 NIV). Does Jesus watch the offering basket today?

The Old Testament priests always knew who was bringing in sacrifices for the Temple. In fact, they inspected them and rejected all defective gifts. They made sure the sacrifices were worthy. The ministers were watchful over the offerings. People had a relationship with their priests. The covenant of God through the tithe connected the ministry and the people together. The blessing of the anointing flowed down. Today, people experience the solitude of a stained-glass sanctuary and call it worship. They have a relationship with a building and think they're in the church. We need to restore personal relationships in the Body of Christ, don't we?

Buildings can't care for your soul. Distant TV preachers can't counsel you or hold you accountable. Religious organizations don't know your needs. Sheep deserve a shepherd. Disciples need a spiritual father. A genuine shepherd prays for your soul and feeds you God's word. He knows his sheep and loves them.

Tithing honors your relationship with your pastor or priest. Tithes are primarily meant to support the service of those who preach the Word of God and pray for your soul. Sometimes, when I had the opportunity, I put my tithe check right into my pastor's hand, looked him in the eye, and say, "God bless you and prosper you!" He gave me pastoral care and fed me from the word. I appreciated it and didn't take it for granted. Now, I don't relate to a pastor anymore but to an apostle. I like to put my tithes into the hands of the apostle who leads our ministry team which I relate to. I bless him with my tithes, with gratitude.

Tithing is recognition of God's care. In fact, *wherever* you pay your tithe indicates your source of covering in Christ. That's where you are accountable. According to Paul, this is the pattern our Lord Jesus taught: (1 Cor. 9:7 NIV) *"Who serves as a soldier at his own expense? Who plants a vineyard and does not eat of its grapes? Who tends a flock and does not drink of the milk?"* and verse 14: *"In the same way, the Lord has commanded that those who preach the gospel should receive their living from the gospel."*

Tithes help fulfill God's ultimate purpose—evangelism. God loves lost souls! God wants more preachers. Invariably, we get what we pay for. Tithing is God's universal method of financing the spread of the gospel. Giving to support Christ's ministry helps more people be saved and more workers be sent.

Tithing is also an act of submission to Christ's authority. By honoring the Lord with your first fruits you are forcing "unrighteous mammon" (money or riches) to become righteous. You are making money serve God rather than serve the world. Money must be made to bow down before God. Money won't serve God unless you force it to. Tithing is the beginning of obedience in financial matters. It opens the door for God's blessings on your whole budget.

How a church handles its money deeply affects its destiny. One major reason why many churches have dried up and lost their blessing is that they have starved their pastors, stoned their prophets, or rejected their apostles. They have withheld the reward that was due the worker. In so doing, they angered God and hurt their flock.

When we muzzle the oxen threshing out the grain, the whole house eventually goes lacking for food. We need to learn a better way, a way that provides both for the preachers and the church. The Bible doesn't leave this issue to guesswork.

Handling money was a critical issue with the Old Testament prophets and the New Testament apostles. What is the Spirit saying to the churches today about handling money? New revenue streams are developing for God's mobile ministers: apostles and prophets.

The prophet Malachi wrote a whole book on tithes and offerings. It appears last in the Old Testament. When Malachi says, *"Bring in the tithes and offerings so that there may be meat in my house..."* (KJV) he was talking about literal meat, offerings, or food for the priests. God wanted his servants to prosper. God wanted the priests to be devoted to the ministry full-time. In the Old Testament, the tithe was brought into the storehouse. The concept of the storehouse is an important aspect of stewarding the tithe. What was the storehouse?

Evicting the Thief

WHAT WAS THE STOREHOUSE? In the Old Testament days of Malachi, the storehouse was a room adjacent to the Temple where contributions were stored. This was a special storage chamber, a storeroom managed by the priests for the priests (Nehemiah 10:37). It wasn't a religious term; it was a real place. You might call it a pantry or a treasury. Today it might be comparable to a warehouse or even a bank account. Here, the priests stored up the grain offerings brought in by the people as gifts to God.

From the storehouse, the priests who served the temple could come and take whatever they needed for themselves and their families. The storehouse wasn't a church treasury controlled by some backslidden Tobiah-type character.

Tobiah is worth examining. His life can tell us a lot about what *not* to do.

During the rebuilding of the walls of Jerusalem, just prior to Israel's return from captivity in Babylon, Tobiah showed up as the chief opponent of the great reformer, Nehemiah. Nehemiah was a *rebuilder*. Any person who wants to achieve great goals and manage organizations should study Nehemiah.

Nehemiah was a noble man in the Bible. He promoted revival. He was a man of prayer and principle. But opposing him was Tobiah. He didn't want revival. He resisted change. He discouraged the laborers. Tobiah was an enemy of renewal. He conspired to maintain control, to keep the status quo; to defeat the workers on the wall. Under Nehemiah's ministry of restoration, it was soon discovered that Tobiah was living in the priests' storeroom.

"Before this, Eliashib the priest had been put in charge of the storerooms of the house of our God. He was closely associated with Tobiah, and he had provided him with a large room formerly used to store the grain offerings and incense and temple articles, and also the tithes of grain, new wine and oil prescribed for the Levites, singers and gatekeepers, as well as the contributions for the priests." (Neh. 13:4-5)

Toby, the Trouble-Maker

A usurper, Tobiah, was occupying a holy place. No wonder the priests were forced to leave the ministry and go tend fields for food—their storehouse was taken over. The priests had no pantry. A holy place had become secular, not sacred. When the preachers or prophets or priests are rejected, God's people languish in captivity.

Nehemiah was angry at this development. Sometimes we have to get mad to get motivated. He drove Tobiah out, dumped his belongings in the street, reinstated the collection of offerings, and appointed a priest to administrate the tithes. He made Tobiah homeless. He revised the revenue stream for God's servants. The scene is reminiscent of Jesus throwing the money-changers out of the Temple (Matthew 21:12). An angry Jesus purged the temple and purified its purpose, which was prayer. Nehemiah reacted in the same strong way.

There are too many Tobiahs controlling church treasuries today. The "Tobiah spirit" discourages the builders, resists revival, undermines God's divine order, and sits in unauthorized offices. The result of tolerating Tobiah is that God's workers are robbed of their wages and God's work goes lacking. It also means that God's delegated leaders are made powerless and penniless.

Who was in charge of the storehouse? God didn't appoint Tobiah to that place. Somebody's *unholy alliance* with Tobiah permitted him to interfere with God's plan. Somebody compromised. Somebody made covenant with an enemy of righteousness. Someone robbed God and defrauded the workers. This nasty situation had to be cleansed before restoration could be accomplished.

We are not authorized to come up with creative ways to rule the money. God's way is the only way because it is the right way. Everything in the storehouse belonged to the servants of God. It didn't belong to anyone except those separated unto the work (commissioned, ordained by God, anointed). Anyone not ordained by God who touched the tithe was cursed by God.

Nehemiah took drastic action. Nehemiah represents God's apostolic fathers and prophetic forerunners of our day, rebuilding and restoring God's temple. He forcefully evicted Tobiah. Nehemiah the prophet stood for God's word and God's ways. He was willing to be disliked by the Tobiah crowd. Are we of the same opinion?

Strong action was called for. Notice what Nehemiah the Reformer did. It is recorded for all time in the Bible. God remembers with favor what this man of God did.

"Here I learned about the evil thing Eliashib had done in providing Tobiah a room in the courts of the house of God. I was greatly displeased and threw all Tobiah's household goods out of the room. I gave orders to purify the rooms, and then I put back into them the equipment of the house of God, with the grain offerings and the incense. I also learned that the portions assigned to the Levites had not been given to them, and that all the Levites and singers responsible for the service had gone back to their own fields. So I rebuked the officials and asked them, "Why is the house of God neglected?" Then I called them together and stationed them at their posts. All Judah brought the tithes of grain, new wine and oil into the storerooms. I put Shelemiah the priest, Zadok the scribe, and a Levite named Pedaiah in charge of the storerooms and made Hanan son of Zaccur, the son of Mattaniah, their assistant, because these men were considered trustworthy. They were made responsible for distributing the supplies to their brothers. Remember me for this, O my God, and do not blot out what I have so faithfully done for the house of my God and its services." (Nehemiah 13:7-14)

When laymen like Tobiah exercise control over the finances of a church or ministry, they usurp the privilege God has reserved to the ministry. The violate divine order. By default, they exercise control over the church's direction. This is out of order. The church's direction should be determined by those called and commissioned of God to lead the church. This refers to apostles and the elders they appoint.

Biblically, the storehouse is the place where the wages of God's workers are stored. The storehouse can be people, the Five-fold ministers listed in Eph. 4:11. The storehouse is the place with reserves where they can go get what they need. If they can't get it, then it is not theirs, not devoted to God.

God is not unjust to reward the labor of love of his servants. In Matthew 20:1-16, Jesus said the kingdom of heaven is like this: workers are hired for the vineyard with wages agreed on first. Their payment came at the end of the day. The story shows that God is just, but not equal. The last workers of the day got the same as the first, but it seemed more when compared to the first workers. God was more generous than anyone expected.

Who determined their wages? The one who hired them, the owner of the field. God pays good wages. Wages should not be withheld. God said in Malachi 3:5, *"So I will come near to you for judgment. I will be quick to testify against sorcerers, adulterers and perjurers, against* **those who defraud laborers of their wages,** *who oppress the widows and the fatherless, and deprive aliens of justice, but do not fear me, says the LORD Almighty."* Defrauding someone of their wages is serious.

Jesus had no problem paying the wages of those he sent out. Study Matthew 10:10. You'll see that he expected his sent ones to be received by those to whom they ministered. *To be received* means more than a handshake and a smile—it means to be financially provided for. If someone is not received, if their message was ignored, if they were disrespected, they were to shake the dust off their feet and move on. The needs of the workers were to be met by those to whom they preached. That's God's pattern.

This pattern is still in effect today. Jesus said we are to pray and ask for God to send out workers into his harvest. When God answers this prayer, we will need to support them. *"The worker is worthy of his support."* Jesus told them not to save up to finance their own ministry but to expect wages. Jesus' instructions were clear—if they don't receive you, go elsewhere. Why? Because God says his workers are worth it. *Generosity* is a sign that the ground has opened up, ready to receive the seed of the word. When the hearts of the people are open, they are worthy of the gospel.

Any move of God, until accompanied by a restoration of financial obedience, is just a flash in the pan. Repentance is only empty religious talk if it doesn't affect our finances.

Indeed, we need to put our money where our mouth is. Or, as one preacher said, "When I baptize converts, I want them to leave their wallets in their pants!"

Revival must include turning back to God with our finances. If we want revival to persist, we must obey God's laws about money. Withholding the tithes and offerings short-circuits revival. We are under an illusion is we think modern revivals can bypass this fundamental law. The great reformers of the Bible paid attention to the elementary principle that worshiping God required honoring him by our giving.

Ezra was such a reformer. He worked along with Nehemiah the scribe and the prophets Zechariah and Haggai. They restored the Temple in Jerusalem after Cyrus issued his decree for the Jews to return from captivity to Israel.

Ezra made sure that the priests were properly supported by tithes and offerings. They rebuilt the altar first, then began work on the temple and the walls.

Why did they build the altar first? An altar is a place where offerings can be brought. They knew that an altar of burnt offerings would invoke God's protection against their enemies. They were terrified of the peoples of the land (Ezra 3:3). How about you? Are your enemies making you fearful? Find an altar!

They rebuilt everything using freewill offerings, but assigned the tithes to those who were proven to be genuine priests (Ezra 2:61-63). In fact, Ezra, the governor, prohibited anyone but priests from partaking of the "holy things."

Rebuilding requires restoring the altar first. That's why I am writing this book; I have a burden for restoration. I want nothing to prevent the outpouring of glory God has destined for the church in these last days.

Building the Church Today

Think with me about this issue. When Paul wanted to demonstrate for New Testament saints how to support the work of the church, what model did he appeal to? He explicitly used the Old Testament pattern of priests in the temple— *"...those who work in the temple get their food from the temple..."* He took a Jewish model and applied it to Gentile converts. Notice his line of reasoning and his conclusions.

"Am I not free? Am I not an apostle? Have I not seen Jesus our Lord? Are you not the result of my work in the Lord? Even though I may not be an apostle to others surely I am to you! For you are the seal of my apostleship in the Lord. This is my defense to those who sit in judgment on me. Don't we have the right to food and drink? Don't we have the right to take a believing wife along with us, as do the other apostles and the Lord's brothers and Cephas? Or is it only I and Barnabas who must work for a living? Who serves as a soldier at his own expense? Who plants a vineyard and does not eat of its grapes? Who tends a flock and does not drink of the milk? Do I say this merely from a human point of view? Doesn't the Law say the same thing? For it is written in the Law of Moses: "Do not muzzle an ox while it is treading out the grain." Is it about oxen that God is concerned? Surely, he says this for us, doesn't he? Yes, this was written for us, because when the plowman plows and the thresher threshes, they ought to do so in the hope of sharing in the harvest. If we have sown spiritual seed among you, is it too much if we reap a material harvest from you? If others have this right of support from you, shouldn't we have it all the more? But we did not use this right. On the contrary, we put up with anything rather than hinder the gospel of Christ. Don't you know that those who work in the temple get their food from the temple, and those who serve at the altar share in what is offered on the altar? In the same way, the Lord has commanded that those who preach the gospel should receive their living from the gospel" 1 Cor 9:1-

14 (NIV). We will come back to this passage later.

Those who serve the altar share in what is offered at the altar. This is Paul's New Testament way of stating the Old Testament doctrine that the tithe belongs to the Levites. It is an eternal truth. Paul specifically applied this doctrine to those who were full-time servants devoted to the ministry of the gospel; apostles and their travelling teams.

The tithe always has and always will have only one use—to supply the livelihood of those God has called and set apart for his work. No other use is authorized in the Bible. Paul particularly and explicitly applied this principle to apostles. Apostles, God's "sent ones," are meant to be supported in their work. The tithe is their inheritance.

Let's look at just one passage among many which shows this pattern very clearly. In Ezekiel 44:28-30, the prophet is picturing a future restored temple and discussing the Levites and the obligation the people have to support them: *"I am to be the only inheritance the priests have. You are to give them no possession in Israel; I will be their possession. They will eat the grain offerings, the sin offerings and the guilt offerings; and everything in Israel **devoted** to the LORD will belong to them. The best of all the firstfruits and of all your special gifts will belong to the priests. You are to give them the first portion of your ground meal so that a blessing may rest on your household"* (NIV- emphasis added)

The tithe is devoted to the Lord and the Lord's servants—this means modern apostles and prophets—who are just as devoted to the Lord as were the priests.

God wants a blessing to rest on our house. Isn't that a wonderful thing to know? How do we realize that blessing? God has a plan. By participating in this plan, you can cause a blessing to come on your own house. You do it by bringing God's portion—the best and the first of your offerings—and giving it to the servant of God. In the Old Testament, this was primarily the priests or the prophets. In the New Testament era, it is the Five-fold ministers. This is an amazing principle. The prosperity of the priest was connected to the prosperity of the people, and vice-versa. Paul the apostle, who travelled and had a big retinue of mobile workers with him, applauded those who partnered with him by their regular financial gifts. (see Phil. 4:10-20)

God said that "devoted" things were intended for the inheritance of the Levites. Devoted things were the best and the first that Israel had to offer. Doing the right thing with devoted things invoked a blessing on their families.

The word "blessing" summarizes all the benefits of the covenant. We can enter into the blessings God had for Abraham by honoring God with our tithes and offerings, not with just one occasional act of charity or one initial deed, but with a lifestyle of faith and obedience to God.

I have emphasized that the tithe is holy unto the Lord. Just what does this mean? As I said, "holy" means set apart for someone's exclusive use, or sanctified. My wife is holy unto me and I am holy unto her. She and I are exclusively for one another and no one else. We are set apart for one another by a covenant.

When a Curse is Loosed

Giving offerings can be a means of great blessings. Offerings are what we give in addition to tithes. *"Whatever your lips utter you must be sure to do, because you made your vow freely to the LORD your God with your own mouth"* (Deuteronomy 23:23).

Offerings can be a solemn promise, an oath, what we vow to God. They are pledges or gifts. It is biblical to make a vow to God, a promise to give, based on faith. A vow is an oath which has been spoken aloud, a stated intention that God ore others can hear. You have given your word when you have spoken an oath. An offering confirmed by an oath can be an excuse, a basis, for God to bless you in an extraordinary way.

"I will come to your temple with burnt offerings and fulfill my vows to you—vows my lips promised and my mouth spoke when I was in trouble.... surely God has listened and heard my voice in prayer." (Psalms 66:13-19 NIV).

God listens to our vows. When we keep our word and fulfill our vows to God, it becomes an occasion for God's righteous vindication. He puts our enemies to flight and rewards us according to our righteousness. It gives God a legal excuse to bless you and a basis to judge your enemy. Making a vow (an oath, a pledge) is a powerful spiritual tool but be careful, because God takes your words seriously. Don't make foolish vows.

Offerings made as faith-pledges can be the secret to breaking out of poverty's grip. A vow can be an instrument to break off a curse or cancel a judgment. A sacrificial gift can end a season of disaster.

David used this method of making a special offering to halt the judgment of God due to his sin. David had sinned by numbering Israel. He failed to heed God's word, that any time Israel was numbered, they had to give a contribution.

"When you take a census of the Israelites to count them, each one must pay the LORD a ransom for his life at the time he is counted. Then no plague will come on them when you number them." (Ex 30:12 NIV)

A plague broke out. He needed to find a way to end the judgment. "David said to him, 'Let me have the site of your threshing floor so I can build an altar to the LORD, that the plague on the people may be stopped. Sell it to me at the full price.'"

Araunah said to David, 'Take it! Let my lord the king do

whatever pleases him. Look, I will give the oxen for the burnt offerings, the threshing sledges for the wood, and the wheat for the grain offering. I will give all this.'

But King David replied to Araunah, 'No, I insist on paying the full price. I will not take for the LORD what is yours, or sacrifice a burnt offering that costs me nothing.'

So, David paid Araunah six hundred shekels of gold for the site.

David built an altar to the LORD there and sacrificed burnt offerings and fellowship offerings. He called on the LORD, and the LORD answered him with fire from heaven on the altar of burnt offering." (1 Chronicles 21:17-26 NIV)

This time of judgment ended. Later the house of God was built on the site of the threshing floor. The Temple of Solomon, began under David, was built on the very place where a sacrifice was made. Miracles happen when people move in faith to sow a seed out of their need. A disaster was turned around. An oath or sacrifice to God can save lives.

Seed must be a freewill offering, something that costs you, something within our power to freely give.

Remember, there is a difference between tithes and offerings. Offerings go for ministry in distant places or to assist the poor or to erect houses of worship. Offerings enable us to practice generosity by sowing into God's people and God's purposes. This is especially true in the realm of missions and of helping the poor. But tithes are meant to meet the needs of those who care for your soul or who proclaim God's word.

That means if you are a local church member, your tithes should go into the house church or the congregation where you receive pastoral care. If you are a house church leader or elder or if you are the pastor of a congregation, your tithes should go into the apostle and his ministry team.

It ought to flow into the ministry where you have a relationship. You defraud the worker when you eat the spiritual food he serves you but keep back the portion due to him, the tithe.

The church is like a family and it is also a spiritual house. A house (Greek, *oikos,* or an economic entity) can be your family, a household, or a community of people such as a tribe. What if a house is violating God's word? Achan was judged and his whole family died for his sin. What was his sin? He was charged with two things: <u>stealing</u> and <u>deceiving</u>. These two things bring a curse upon the transgressor. This was borne out by the words of the prophet Zechariah:

"Then he said to me, 'This is the curse that is going forth over the face of the whole land; surely everyone who steals will be purged away according to the writing on one side, and everyone who swears will be purged away according to the writing on the other side. I will make it go forth,' declares the LORD of hosts, 'and it will enter the house of the thief and the house of the one who swears falsely by My name; and it will spend the night within that house and consume it with its timber and stones'" (Zechariah 5:3-4 NASB). To "swear" means to answer falsely, to deceive.

This curse was released to go throughout the land and to rest on the house of the thief and the liar. This principle of God is still in effect today. The power of God's word is inexorably sweeping across nations. It is a force that cannot be halted.

It is no coincidence that an upturn of economic global prosperity is often followed by a worldwide shaking of financial markets. Why? Because the nations usually have not honored God with their wealth. One day, that will change.

The word "curse" is a very strong word. It appears over

200 times in the Bible. Moses warned God's people by saying that they have the power to choose blessings or curses, based on their response to God's word (see Dt. 28:2, 12, 15, 25 and Dt. 30:15, 25). Moses said God's people could choose to be blessed or decide to be cursed based on their obedience, or lack of it. When God speaks, pay attention!

The curse announced by Zechariah was written on two sides of a scroll containing a decree from God. It was to come upon an individual and affect his entire family. According to different translations, it was to *"enter his house," "spend the night in his house,"* or *"remain in his house."* Would you like a curse to live in your house, even for one night? Not me!

Who does this curse come upon? The one who *steals* and the one who *lies*. When do you suppose Christians are most guilty of committing these sins? When we misrepresent our offerings as tithes.

How does this curse affect a person? He will be "taken away" and his house will be "destroyed." To be taken away means to be cut off or to be banished. That means he will lose his place among God's people. The destruction of the house means it will be consumed. That means his household will come to chaos and ruin.

I have seen many moms and dads whose families came into confusion and lawlessness and the root of it was the sin of dishonoring God. The walls of protection were torn down and the enemy stole their children away or even led them into divorce and backsliding.

In the same way, the church today will be defeated before the devil and will be powerless before the world if we don't sanctify the tithe in the house of God. The key to victory for Israel in that day is the same for us today. The church needs to enter its inheritance. To take possession of the land, we need divine authority to drive out the opposing spiritual enemies. We must be right with God.

For generations, the religious world has had only pastors and a few teachers. Sadly, the primary ministries named in the Bible, apostles and prophets, have been neglected. These ministries are the reformers. They deal with fundamental doctrines, spiritual warfare, strategic ministries, and they lay correct foundations.

The modern foundation ministries God is raising up today need strong revenue streams to succeed.

God's presence in our midst is requiring holiness in our offerings. We are moving away from religious traditions to a rediscovery of an apostolic paradigm regarding finances.

What if some ministers abuse their privileges and misuse tithes and offerings? What if some leaders prove unworthy of this trust? As apostle Ron McGee once told me, "God gives every minister the right to destroy his own ministry." Integrity is required. This is best done with alignment and accountability.

God is raising up a new breed of laborers, those who have seen the crucified Lord and have despised their own flesh, who can be trusted with the gifts of the Holy Spirit and with the financial resources necessary to fulfill their mission. If we understand God's plan, we can cooperate with his program.

Honor God's Servants

DISHONOR IS RAMPANT in modern American culture. You can see it first in the family, in school kids, and in many churches. God says to honor our father and mother. Honor the elderly. Honor leaders and ministers. Because we fail to train the next generation how to honor, we get the opposite.

God's kingdom is a new society wherein dwells honor for all. The preaching of the kingdom the examples of our leaders, and the teaching from the scriptures should create a counter-culture to the ways of this modern age. We are especially told to honor our leaders. Honor has monetary implications. The Bible teaches that those who are devoted to the ministry of the word are worth twice the salary.

1 Timothy 5:17-18 says, "The elders who direct the affairs of the church well are worthy of double honor..." and "don't muzzle the ox."

"Elders" refers to the pastoral leaders who oversee the church. "Double honor" means double the salary. Honor means manifested esteem and material rewards. To "muzzle the ox" means to keep him from partaking of what he is producing; to choke off his supply.

For example, when the Bible says to honor our father and our mother, it means more than words of respect. It means we must be responsible for their financial security in their old age. (Mark 7:11-13) I had the honor of fulfilling some of that role for my infirm and elderly father for many years until he died. Honor cannot be merely words or applause. It must have substance.

Honor is *manifested esteem.* It must be demonstrated in tangible ways. If honor isn't shown in material ways, then it is merely empty lip service, words without actions, empty of content. King David could have offered up a sacrifice, a field he could have had at no cost, but he refused. Why? He knew that honor toward God had to cost him something. (2 Samuel 24:24)

Those who lead the church wisely and minister the word through preaching and teaching are worthy of generous compensation. Whatever system we use to measure how tithes are spent to compensate ministers, we must not violate this firm biblical principle: *Don't muzzle the ox who is treading out the grain.* Apostles who teach God's word and model God's ways are God's oxen. Their labor produces food for God's people. They have a right to partake of what their ministry produces.

You see, there are three levels of giving associated with supporting the work of God being done by his servants.

The first is **wages**. That means the laborer is worthy of his hire. James 5:4 warns of heavenly judgment for this financial sin. If we don't do at least this minimum, then we have defrauded the worker and we will anger God. Wages are earned. If we fail to render what is due when it is due, we are guilty of robbery. Delay in making payment is a sin.

The second level is **honor**. Honor is always done as unto the Lord. It goes way beyond what anyone deserves as pay. (1 Tim. 5:17) It is not *quid pro quo* for services rendered; instead it is an honorarium because we have respect for the Lord who sent his servant to us. Honor is given because of someone's office or because of Who they represent. We honor them and the Lord as we give.

It is right to distinguish degrees of honor that are due someone for their calling or gifting, their experience, or their maturity and years of labor. Even in secular society, we give more honor to those whose expertise is more valuable. In this regard, experienced apostles are worthy of more honor than pastors. Those leading a network of churches are due more honor than those leading only one church. Those leading a congregation of hundreds is worthy of more honor than someone leading a house church of only a dozen souls.

The third level is **sowing**. This is when we participate with God's servant in the work they are doing. We partner with them in the task of taking the gospel to new areas. We help them evangelize or plant churches. (2 Cor 9:9-15) We are joined to these teams in the gospel work and get to share in their reward. Sowing occurs when we invest with an expectation of seeing a harvest. Usually, we sow into a vision by supporting an expansive word or launching a new work.

Robert Trask of the Assemblies of God has said, *"Every church ought to be a parent or a partner in church planting."*

To summarize these three levels of giving:

- Wages are what is due the worker.
- Honor is for the Lord who sent them.
- Sowing is for the harvest to increase.

God is concerned for the work, but he also cares for the worker. The pattern for most of God's servants in the Bible is that they personally prospered. Moses, Abraham, David, and Solomon all had wealth. Most also went through great trials on the way to success. Jesus fed thousands and supported a ministry team as they travelled. He even had a team treasurer, Judas. He had access to riches, but he became poor so that we could share his riches. *"For you know the grace of our Lord Jesus Christ, that though he was rich, yet for your sakes he became poor, so that you through his poverty might become rich."* (2 Corinthians 8:9 NIV).

The cross is the basis for God exchanging our poverty for his prosperity. As the late Bible teacher Derek Prince said, *"Christ exhausted the curse of sin, poverty, and sickness on the cross for our benefit."*

Judas was Jesus' treasurer (John 13:29). He complained because Jesus received extravagant offerings, but was always giving money to the poor. Jesus had funds, yet he wasn't broke. He always had money to give away. That's why Jesus never ran out of money—he was continually sowing into the powerless and the Father kept repaying him.

This doesn't mean God's servants in the Bible were never tested in their finances. It is not uncommon for God to work humility and perseverance into the character of his leaders before trusting them with power, revelation, influence, or wealth. Faith must be tested. Then it becomes like gold.

Motives get quickly revealed during poverty *or* prosperity. Either extreme can produce a real test of faith or character. The apostle Paul said he had learned how to be abased and how to abound. Many a man has become wealthy only to lose it after he decided, "I can't tithe that much."

Bob Wilhite, in his excellent book *Why Pray?* makes the point that selfishness is idolatry. He says that material wealth which comes to Christians will test their character and integrity. This is true. Our riches (wealth) are first and foremost heavenly riches. But the modern church has forgotten that it is God's blessings, coupled with diligence and dedicated labor, that make us materially rich. Even the ideas that we capitalize upon to succeed: those also came from God. We may be jealous of, suspicious of, or prejudiced against Christians who have prospered. Don't do it.

"Frequently the church misses it in how we treat God's servants," said my late friend, apostle Bob Terrell. Bob had been a Master Sargent in the Army. A big bear of a man, when he got saved, he became sold out to Jesus. He planted many churches, oversaw a network of house churches, consulted with many pastors, made disciples, and flowed with the knowledge of the Lord and his ways. He walked in great spiritual authority. I loved him. He is in heaven now.

Somehow, we equate poverty with humility. Sadly, the famine of God's word in many churches can often be traced to the habit of depriving God's servants of their due reward. Lean ministers produce lean portions for the flock. Payday arrives when what we have sowed, we begin to reap.

God isn't stingy with his servants. He wants them to be well cared for. *"And let them say continually, 'The Lord be magnified!' Who delights in the prosperity of his servant"* (Psalms 35:27). God is pleased for his servants to prosper and he wants them to rejoice in abundance.

How do God's servants prosper? Through receiving tithes and offerings, funds which are paid by God's people to the support of their apostles, prophets, or teachers. Scripturally, tithes belong to the full-time workers devoted to God's service. *"...for the Levites are they who receive the tithes...thus we will not neglect the house of our God."* (Nehemiah 10:37)

A modern church practice has been to subvert the tithe to a lesser use, that is, to build religious auditoriums. At first glance, this seems acceptable. But it can be a dangerous departure from the biblical pattern. These buildings can become monuments to movements that once knew God's glory. Unless God's glory is truly there, it's just an empty house.

One thing is undeniable—in the Bible, tithes were *never* used to construct houses of worship. Sorry, but that's a fact. I'm not saying you can't ever do it. I'm just saying that it isn't the model taught in the Scriptures. In the New Testament, the tithes, after the Day of Pentecost, supported apostles, and later, their roving ministry teams.

David didn't Rob the Priests to Build the Temple

David built the Temple with freewill offerings, not the sacred tithe (See 1 Chronicles 29). David knew the tithes were sanctified. David didn't rob the priests of their tithes to build the Temple. But many churches have done just that. Understand, I'm not against buildings. They are a practical necessity in developed countries. But they have also become a substitute for genuine church growth. Modern Christian thinking equates buildings with the Body of Christ. That is an error. The church is the people, not the property.

For the first 300 years of Christianity, the church met in homes, much like modern cell groups or like John Wesley's small classes. The real church, both then and now, is the people, the *ecclesia*. (Ephesians 2:19-22) The church is composed of the saints assembled under Christ's authority, not a building on a street corner. Yet good buildings in good locations can help a church impact a community.

What are the needs of the ministry? What are the needs of the flock? What can you afford? Don't rush to build a structure as a monument to somebody's ego just because you don't have anything better to do with the money. Invest it in multiplying the ministry of the word as a priority. Send out workers. Then, use wisdom when you build. If possible, build debt-free, using offerings.

Generally, I think, we should *initially erect* houses of worship with offerings, be debt free, and then *maintain* them out of a small portion of the tithes, yet without ever depriving the preachers. Let's keep the biblical distinction of these two categories of giving: tithes and offerings.

The pattern established by David (and by Moses before him) was that the construction of the temple or tabernacle or house of worship came from special offerings. In fact, their giving was so generous that they had to be restrained from bringing any more gifts during the construction phase. (Exodus 36:5)

After the temple was completed, the priests cared for all the maintenance and operating costs from the offerings which they routinely received. There also was an annual "temple tax" by the people toward this facility expense. What is quite clear is that they didn't build the house of God with tithes but with special contributions.

Reject Lame Sacrifices

A friend of mine, Ron McGee, is the founding pastor of a church in North Carolina called The Rock of Wilmington. He told me this story about a "lame sacrifice." It is a tale that is repeated too often. It illustrates the culture of dishonor that has permeated modern Christianity.

At the time of this incident, Ron and his wife were pastoring a small church in Georgia. In it was a wealthy businessman. This man alone, if he had been tithing faithfully, could have made a huge difference in that church's success. Ron and his wife were laboring to see the church grow but their salary was meager. They were struggling.

One day, the door-bell rang. The rich man and his well-dressed wife stood at the door. They were holding a large package. Ron's heart leaped with hope. "They've come to bless us!"

As he opened the door, the rich man handed Ron the package and said, "Preacher, this meat we had in our freezer is freezer-burned. We don't want it anymore. If you'll cut the bad parts off, it's still good enough to eat. We just wanted to give something to the Lord. Bless y'all, now!"

Needless to say, pastor Ron threw the meat in the garbage. How would you have felt if you had been him?

My friend learned a vital lesson from that humiliating experience. Later, he moved on to plant a new church with new values. There, he faithfully taught the apostolic principle of the tithe. In his teaching, he says that God deserves the first and the best of anything we offer to him. He says that we ought to pay our tithes without any strings attached, trusting God's leaders to spend it wisely. The result is that Ron's church members, trained through Covenant Classes, have learned to show honor to the Lord and to the Lord's servants. They even break out into spontaneous applause at offering time!

From my observations, their church has an abundance for its work. Their new congregation retired the mortgage on their first building in seven years. They are giving large amounts of money to missions and local charity. They expanded and built a lovely campus on 80 acres.

This church glorifies God with their finances. They help the poor. They are generous with guest speakers. They treat their pastors and staff well. Their church is filled with people who are experiencing God's blessings on their families and their finances. None of this happened by accident, but because their pastor, apostle Ron, determined to teach the scriptures about the tithe. He deliberately taught God's word to create a culture of honor toward the Lord and toward God's servants. He laid a solid foundation.

In my judgement, knowing Ron McGee personally, his courage to do this occurred because he feared God more than he feared the opinions of the people.

At a certain point in my ministry I was invited to become senior pastor of a church whose founder was ailing and desiring to retire. After taking the reins of leadership, I made the unsettling discovery that only about 25% of the membership was tithing.

The pastor had been proud of the fact that he never emphasized money. He adopted the practice of having a small box hung on the back wall of the auditorium, so people could discretely drop in their checks as they left. The problem was this: they were leaving tips, not tithes. That way of receiving money wasn't the real issue, although I personally prefer celebrating joyfully as we give to God. The issue was honor, or the lack of it.

As soon as I saw what was happening, I was alarmed. I took the church giving records of the people and went alone into the auditorium. I laid on my face before God in intercession. I pleaded with the Lord, saying, *"God, if you will give me time, I will fix this. Please forgive this church for robbing you."* Then, I began to teach that the tithe was holy unto the Lord.

Within two months, the church's monthly giving had tripled! We started celebrating giving to God. A lame church quit limping along and we were able to grow with God's blessings.

Tithes are precious to God. In Deuteronomy 26:8-19, God describes giving the tithe as an act of worship. To worship means "to adore someone." God's obedient people could vow, saying, *"I have removed the sacred portion from my house and have given it to the Levite..."* Being able to make that statement is powerful. It silences the accuser.

The tithe is a sacred portion. Remember, the word *sacred* means "holy." Bringing your tithes to the Lord is an act of adoration, a form of worship done in a material way, a sacrifice that costs you something. The tithe is not an idea you believe in—it is an act you perform. It counts with God.

We must *do* something with the tithe. The Scripture

says the tithe is to be taken out of my house and put into the hands of God's servant in the house of the Lord. That means I give up control over it. I have no say over its use. I release it with no strings attached. I relinquish it to God's servant.

He shouldn't have to come to me and beg for it. It is my job two give it; not his job to collect it. I should bring it as an offering of love, as an act of worship done in faith and devotion, with respect and honor.

America is Rich

Compared to the rest of the world, the American church is rich. Even if the church treasury is low, the people sitting on the pews are prosperous. Therefore, the church is not broke. The church is the people, not its treasury. In America, the median income in 1997 was $37,000. Americans gave $24 billion to charity in 1997. Americans also spent $24 billion on magazines that same year. We are a wealthy nation.

Yet among adults who attend church at least once per month, over one-third (37%) gave no money at all. Of those who do give, the national average is only 3% of their income. The average weekly donation among Protestants is just $17. This is pitiful.

Those who tithe (that is, give 10% of their income to the church) account for only 3-5% of all givers in typical American churches. This is a shame. Somebody isn't teaching the church the whole truth in the Bible.

In giving, there is not much of a difference among denominations. Among people who gave *any* amount at all during the previous 12 months, the ranking looked like this: Presbyterians- 63%; Church of Christ- 61%; Assembly of God- 60%; Nondenominational- 59%; Lutherans- 58%; Methodists- 56%; Baptists- 48%; Catholics- 47%;

Pentecostal- 47%; Episcopal- 46%. Statistics quoted here are from a reliable professional pollster.[10]

To look at it another way, this means 37% of all Presbyterians gave nothing at all for a whole year, and 40% of Assemblies of God members gave zero in the last twelve months. At least in this area, it looks like we're not doing a very good job of making disciples of our members.

A Reformation is Underway

The exception to this pattern seems to be among those renewed areas of the church known as the new apostolic reformation. Peter Wagner, in his book *The New Apostolic Churches* (Regal, 1998), says that one hallmark of this movement is the churches seem to have abundant finances to fulfill their vision. Three aspects of these churches are:

(1) Generous giving is expected. Wagner says, "Tithing is taught without apology and those who do not tithe their incomes are subtly encouraged to evaluate their Christian lives as sub-par."

(2) Giving is taught as beneficial to the giver. Tithes and offerings are believed to be seed that if given will produce a harvest of like kind in our lives. Luke 6:38 is taken literally.

(3) Giving is cheerful. Wagner says in some of these apostolic churches he has seen the people break out into rousing shouting and clapping the moment the pastor announces it is time to receive the Sunday offering.

We need more apostolic and prophetic voices to be raised up to help local pastors with the problem of low-level participation in the tithe. Sometimes it is difficult for a pastor to address thorny issues in his own church.

---

[10] *How to Increase Giving in Your Church*, George Barna, published by Regal Books.

Wineskins can hurt you. Sheep can bite you. Courage is required. Don't hesitate to get outside help.

Some blessings from God await corporate obedience. I have a friend whose church has a 90% tithe ratio. That is quite an achievement. He was bragging to the Lord about this one day and the Lord said to him, "Why aren't you grieving over the 10% who are robbing Me?"

To make the point, let's look at what it means to defraud someone. What if you, as a pastor, discovered that half the women in your church were refusing to share the marital bed with their husband. What if you found out that the men were ignorant about their duty to pleasure their spouse, or didn't know how to please their wives? I'm sure that you are aware the Bible says couples are not to defraud their partner of intimate fulfillment. (1 Cor. 7:3) Wouldn't you begin to teach the adults in your church how to fix this?

The same is true about financial matters. Train new believers how to honor God by giving consistently.

We need to teach our people what the Bible says about giving. Bible scholar Dr. Peter Wagner said, *"Giving is beneficial to the person who gives."* If for no other reason, we should teach people to give so they will receive the benefits.

An Apostolic Paradigm

HOW DO WE FINANCE the ministry? How does the kingdom of God grow in a practical way? How are workers to be supported for the mission, not just maintenance?

A whole new way of seeing the church is emerging in our day. This topic touches a wonderful area of renewal, the development of apostolic teams and local presbyteries in churches and in cities. Apostolic teams gather around fathers in the faith. These spiritual fathers make disciples, plant churches, and lay the foundation for the church to be built. They oversee networks and operate in collegiality.

Being an apostle is rightly understood to be a job description more than it is an office or a title. There are over 25 men (and one woman) named as apostles in the New Testament. To be apostolic, the church needs apostles. (Rom. 1:5) An apostolic pattern in the church is vigorous, not stagnant. In the New Testament, the book "Acts of the Apostles" shows God's organic model for church growth.

The Bible calls these pioneers or spiritual fathers *apostles*, which means "sent ones." In that sense, anyone sent by God is apostolic, on a mission. They may be known as pastors, teachers, evangelists, or prophets, (Ephesians 4:11), but if they are sent out, then they carry a degree of apostolic grace. They have influence over people in a place or ethnic group. Heaven honors their authority. Their authority will be more effective when recognized within their divinely authorized boundary. Their turf is known and enforced by God's angelic messengers. Evil spirits also know who they are and oppose them.

Can you answer the question, "Do you have a right to be here?" "Who sent you?" "Whose authority are you under?" To function with full power, God's sent ones should be recognized and received by the body of Christ, the church.

I have come to believe that God also authorizes and sends men and women into business or politics with a peculiar and special type of grace to function, succeed. They prosper in that designated non-religious realm. Not all of God's grace-gifts are intended to function inside God's house. The field (the world) also needs God's gifted workers deployed. God's grace works everywhere it is received.

An apostle's team will have a turf, a defined territory. Spiritually, it extends to certain geographic areas via the relationships of those ministers allied with the team. The reach of these teams—their sphere of influence—is usually well beyond that of their local church (See 2 Corinthians 10:13). Apostles are sent to a people or place, on purpose.

Some apostles are "set apart" for the work of strengthening or planting churches. (Acts 13:1-4) They no longer stay in one area like a local pastor, but are mobile ministers. For that reason, they are called trans-local ministries. They don't have a local church paying their salary. They have given up their career or vocation. I believe these apostolic networks are a good biblical alternative to independent churches or to petrified denominationalism.

Why is this relevant to church finances? The emerging

development of apostolic fathers and their mobile ministry teams presents a real challenge to the institutional way of dealing with financial matters in churches. It requires major funding. It may seem threatening to old traditions.

Let's acknowledge that God used historic churches in a wonderful way. Many churches which do not embrace a new apostolic paradigm have nonetheless done a commendable work and blessed many people. They walked in the light they had at the time. Great missionary movements even impacted nations yet they knew little of biblical terminology about apostles. *No one is out to change them if they are content as they are.*

Institutional or denominational church structures have been around a long time, many hundreds of years in some cases, and they aren't going away anytime soon. Let's leave them in peace, but let's obey God.

Traditions have developed in historic churches to deal with the handling of money. Some of these traditions are good but some of them stifle the church's original apostolic and missionary purpose.

In traditional churches that are affiliated with a denomination, a hierarchy of some kind helps to establish a policy which gives churches guidelines for handling money. These guidelines determine where the peoples' giving will be directed: toward the pastor's salary, building programs, maintenance, advertising, mission endeavors, charity, benevolence, literature, denominational headquarters' needs, etc. In addition to guidelines, there are usually safeguards built into the system, some form of check and balance to ensure propriety, to ethically and legally handle donations (more about safeguards later).

Many new independent churches have no such protocol. They develop their own methods which will vary widely depending on the practical business experience of its leaders and depending on their understanding of church government. Often, they borrow models taken from older established churches. Sometimes this results in new wine being put into old wineskins. They should seek counsel from wiser old apostles.

Many evangelical churches have accountability in the vote of the congregation itself. In churches that are independent (most charismatic congregations presently fall into this category), there is often a board or council that develops within the church to provide oversight of the church's finances. The board of laymen and the senior pastor develop an agreement and institute a structure to oversee the finances. This is common in congregationally governed churches.

A new church paradigm has been developing that models biblical or kingdom values which respects the Five-Fold offices (the various post-Ascension ministry gifts of Christ listed in Ephesians 4:11) and honors the tithe as being set apart for those called to the ministry. This new pattern is usually seen in churches being led by a minister who has apostolic grace. Apostolic grace enables a leader to set in foundational truths, raise up spiritual sons, and exercise government or maintain order in a wise fatherly way.

If the senior pastor was the founding apostle of the work, he will usually have more say-so regarding finances than an ordinary pastor or a young preacher. In cases which follow this kind of apostolic pattern, the tithe revenue and church budget are overseen exclusively by the presbytery (the council of elders) and will not normally be subject to any review by the congregation. Wise pastors seek the input of bishops or apostles in these matters.

I have seen this work very well when there is integrity and maturity in the leadership. A key factor in their success is that the church is led by or is within the sphere of an apostle, not just trying to imitate new patterns without relating to someone with a genuine gift of grace to help.

Church business is big business. Excellent stewardship is required. Healthy congregations handle thousands of dollars in donations each month. The people who are giving to the church have a right to know that their contributions are being handled in a legal and business-like manner. It is a violation of ethics to betray their trust. Donors to all non-profit corporations have a right to be assured that the tax-deductible status of their gifts will never be in jeopardy. The Internal Revenue Service will frown upon any organization which fails to fulfill its obligations to keep accurate records and abide by its charter as a religious organization. Genuine churches, whether formally incorporated or not, should work to keep their reputations above reproach.

It doesn't help that some media ministers have abused their privilege of trust. Jim Baker in his book, *I Was Wrong,* details his rise and fall from power due to greed and immorality. Jim had no one around him to tell him the truth, no real accountability. Those who tried, he fired. Celebrity status often is accompanied by arrogance and deception. These few public failures make trouble for the majority who are honest but unnoticed.

The dangers of abuse are always with us. Thus, there needs to be in place a system of financial control and accountability. But there is another danger as well. This danger is that the safeguards will be so stringent that they will choke the vision out of the ministry. Over-control is as much a problem as no control at all. Remember, whoever controls the money, controls the church.

A visionary leader needs some latitude to take initiative. A balance is required. Financial matters must be in the light, open to scrutiny by a trustworthy council. However, the council must be in harmony with the servant of God who is leading the church. Don't muzzle the ox. Don't quench the Spirit. Don't stifle the vision.

A Thief in the Storehouse

As new church systems develop, there is a need for adequate safeguards to protect the church and the ministry from abuses. Sometimes common sense is our best guideline. For example, it makes sense to set an annual salary and pay the pastor a decent wage. The salary must be recorded in the minutes of the church's governing body, either by a board or an eldership. Every church board needs to keep good financial books and record the minutes of all its meetings. This is both a sound business practice and a legal requirement of the IRS for non-profit corporations. We never get so spiritual that we don't need to maintain sound business practices. Write down in the notes what you have agreed to do. God is a God of order, not confusion.

As the Body of Christ goes through Holy Spirit transformation and apostolic renewal, more and more people will discern the office gifts resident in the church. Members will begin to relate to the Five-Fold ministry gifts and not just to the organization or the brand name.

More and more movements are slowly becoming more apostolic in their thinking and methods. God is using prophetic voices (prophets, reformers) to provoke this positive change. Understand, I use the word *apostolic* to describe an aspect of Christ's leadership, a gift or anointing resident in certain Christian leaders who are called and equipped by God.

Relational integrity and apostolic identity is returning to the church. The Body of Christ will be organically linked in relationships to the headship ministries of Ephesians 4:11-16. Every church ought to be connected to the primary foundation gifts—apostles and prophets—and not only to pastors. Every church needs to avail itself of the vision, revelation, wisdom, and authority of these office gifts even if just to observe, audit, advise, or assist the pastoral church leaders.

No matter what ecclesiastical name we call them—

presbyters, superintendents, bishops—it doesn't matter. Titles are not so important: functions are. Do they have the apostolic anointing required to do the job? We need these high-level grace-gifts at work among us. The Great Commission requires "All hands, on deck!" All the gifts and ministries need to be present and accounted for, whether local or mobile.

Apparently, Peter did his apostolic consulting with local elders, referring to himself as a "fellow elder" (Greek: *sum-presbuteros*), as he visited them and sat in council with the elders in the city (1 Pet. 5:1). We need wise counsel, amen?

The revelation of reformed church government is vital as our modern wineskins continue to change as God pours out more of his glory upon the church.

In studying the apostle Paul's relationship with those churches that he ministered to, it is obvious that he taught and practiced financial integrity and principles of sowing and reaping. He wanted all church leaders to be an example of financial integrity, first at home, then at church. The church at Philippi is a case in point of how to partner with an apostle.

Boldness in Sharing

Paul freely solicited offerings from those he served in Philippi. Why? Because he knew it was God's plan. There was a financial partnership between certain churches and his apostolic team. He also knew this bond would meet his needs, so he could focus on his primary work—preaching the gospel, making disciples, and planting churches.

This partnership was the basis for God's blessing increasing on their lives. "But I have received everything in full, and have an abundance; I am amply supplied, having received from Epaphroditus what you have sent, a fragrant aroma, an acceptable sacrifice, well-pleasing to God. And my God shall supply all your needs according to His riches in glory in Christ Jesus." (Phil 4:18-19 NASB).

Their offering was pleasing to God, a fragrant sacrifice on God's altar. In return, Paul said that God was committed to supplying all their needs.

This Scripture is often quoted out of context, as though it was a unilateral promise with no conditions. The promise of abundant provision was not made to everyone but only to those who partnered through their giving. This partnership can function when local churches give seed for sowing to preachers fulfilling a mission to extend God's kingdom.

Another reason Paul was bold about offerings was that he wanted the givers to be blessed. Here is what he said in Philippians 4:17, *"Not because I desire a gift: but I desire fruit that may abound to your account."*

Their act of giving to him and his labor became an instrument of God's righteous reward. God honors giving when it is practiced in faith and love. Depriving people of the opportunity to joyously give to the Lord harms the church.

Paul wasn't afraid to receive an offering. He desired both temporal and eternal profits for those he ministered to. He wanted to see immediate needs being met *and* eternal rewards credited to their account in heaven. This lesson is vital to our success in missions today.

More and more, the final purpose of apostolic and prophetic power, in its maturing (yet still partial) expression of Jesus' present-day ministry, will be more fully unveiled *only* as it turns away from the task of reforming the church and starts addressing the needs of the poor and afflicted, and our mandate to deliver the gospel of the kingdom to every nation. If we don't do this, then we have left a "hole in our gospel" and don't yet have "the whole gospel."

In Philippians, Paul lets us see inside his apostolic network of churches and how his support for missions was generated. Why did the Holy Spirit record this account in our Bible? Does it tell us something about God's delight when churches give generously? God didn't put these promises in the Bible to deceive us or to manipulate us. God keeps his word and he blesses those who give.

Tithes in Cell Groups or House Churches

We are watching emerging apostles in the developing church (see my book of that same title). Mobile ministry teams create a new challenge for supporting the ministry today. For local pastors, with a church building and a settled culture, the issue seems clear. They are deemed legitimate because they have a building and their ministers are "full-time" in the ministry. Is that true? God is creating a new wineskin, not reinforcing old structures. God is establishing new criteria. His apostles, prophets, evangelists, and teachers are not necessarily tied down to a building or to one location. How do we support them? They deserve support because Jesus is sending them to us.

The emergence of apostolic leadership isn't the only thing that is requiring flexibility in our thinking. One of the new models of "doing church" that has developed in the last few decades is the cell church, a global phenomenon and a major success story, even in poor nations.

Cell churches in developed countries often have access to large facilities to accommodate the gathered crowd but their pastoral ministry takes place in the homes of the members. This is a practical and strategic blend of visions. Ted Haggard used the phrase "facility-based cell church" to describe churches that modify their ministry to incorporate cell groups as part of a larger congregation. In Colombia, a network of believers with thousands of house churches has emerged. This system has evangelized thousands of people.

True cell churches are not dependent on buildings for their survival. They can flourish underground if need be, without owning real estate. For this reason, the underground church in China has prospered despite communist oppression. I saw this first-hand in the house-churches in Cuba. The same is true of the growing church in Ethiopia. Many Christians in that nation were martyred and church buildings were burned or confiscated, but the church went underground into cell groups... and multiplied itself. Many Latin American churches have had astounding growth through cells. In most Muslim nations today, secret house churches are the only way they can gather. Low-profile cell churches are better able to handle persecution than public facility-based churches, plus, they reproduce disciples of Jesus more quickly.

How do New Testament cell-based churches handle tithes? In churches that are cell-based, these financial principles of paying tithes, giving offerings, and using tithes for the support of full-time ministers can work exceedingly well. In fact, they are better able to employ more ministers or send out more missionaries because they have so many lay ministers helping to shepherd the flock in the cell meetings. Those who shepherd cell churches don't normally quit their secular vocations. They collect tithes and offerings to distribute to needs that are greater than their own. They can underwrite apostles who travel. They can distribute charity to the poor. Plus, these churches don't have the expense or overhead of buildings. The money from contributions can more readily go to paying gospel workers rather than the prohibitive cost of facilities and property. In most persecuted lands, churches are not allowed to own property.

The key to this concept is understanding relationships, building trust, and honoring God's biblical authority in trusted leaders. Covenantal love thrives in community.

Cell groups and the elders who lead them should never be isolated, separated off unto themselves. They should always be linked to Christ's Five-Fold headship ministries in the city or region, just as members of a body are attached to the spine and to the neck and thus to the head. No little flock should remain isolated from the rest of the church in the city. Cells that are cut off from the rest of the Body of Christ are cult-like. They are out of order. Healthy cells integrate, unite, and function under divine authority. The body of Christ should not be splintered.[11]

There are many cell model churches that seem good. The pattern that I have seen is for the tithes to be devoted to full-time ministers, to support the experienced elders on the pastoral team. Only a small minority of cell group leaders are ever intended by God to become full-time in the ministry. Most are meant to keep their day jobs. We practiced this pattern in a church in which I was an elder in Texas. We grew the church using home meetings long before we bought land and erected a house of worship for the cell churches to congregate.

The full-time ordained workers are meant to be the ones who live by the tithes, not lay workers. God honors secular vocations and blesses his people through their jobs. No one is of lesser value in God's house because they are not devoted to the ministry full-time. One of my favorite people is John Moore. His business card says, "Rancher. Writer. Prophet." Regardless of our job, we serve King Jesus.

Everyone following Jesus has a holy calling in addition to their vocational calling. God's grace places gifts in every believer. All work is holy when done unto the Lord. In other words, "Don't quit your day job." That too, is part of God's kingdom and part of his plan for you.

---

[11] For more on this topic, see *Houses of Prayer in the City*, and *Emerging Apostles in the Developing Church*.

Lay-workers ought to be under the authority of their senior pastor, presiding bishop, or founding apostle. Elders or lay-shepherds who lead cell groups in the church or who direct local ministries will be mostly laymen. Most laymen will never be called on to give up their secular work and its benefits, but should be willing to do so if God requires it. The apostles of Jesus had to do this when they "left their nets and followed him."

Lay leaders of cell groups, if the church goes underground due to persecution, can transmit the tithes of their home flock up the "chain of command" until it arrives in the hands of the presbytery (a leadership council) so it can be distributed to those who are devoted to the work. More and more, it is the mobile ministries (like apostles, prophets, and teachers) who need to be supported by tithes, so they can fulfill their mission.

The tithes need to be placed under the oversight of the elders and pastors in the ministry. Elders will know who their apostle is.

God makes a distinction regarding those set apart for the work (Acts 13), but he doesn't limit who can freely minister their gifts (Romans 12). Everyone is called to use their gifts by faith to serve the Body of Christ (1 Cor. 12-14).

Many powerfully gifted ministers, such as Carlos Annacondia, an evangelist, are successful businessmen. Those with good paying jobs should not charge the church for their time or their ministry. Normally, ministry occurs without salary, unless the task at hand places a demand on the person's time.

Laymen can have a ministry no less real and no less anointed than a full-time worker. Anyone can move into the serving roles listed in Romans 12. Everyone has a measure of grace. Sometimes that grace is intended to prosper a person in a secular vocation. In that realm of business, they have an authority to function and to prosper which comes directly from God. An interesting theology supports this idea, that we are all kings and priests.

Kings and Priests

The Scripture says we are "kings and priests" in Christ. (Rev. 1:6) We are all part of a kingdom of priests, all with direct access to God, all ruling in life by his gift of righteousness. We have differing functions, varied callings, grace-gifts, and measures of faith in our placement in the body of Christ. Rich Marshall, who now travels in ministry, developed this teaching on kings and priests while he was pastor of Springs of Life Fellowship in Sunnyvale, CA.

We as believers are all kings and priests unto God, offering up spiritual sacrifices (1 Peter 2:5). We are royalty, with direct access to God's throne, to pray and praise. In addition, there are some selected by God to serve his word to the church and be a model of kingdom life.

Priests are like the Levites of the Old Testament. They lived off the sacrifices brought to the temple by the people. In the New Testament, these spiritual offices are fulfilled by Christ's Ascension Gift ministries—the apostles, prophets, evangelists, shepherds and teachers.

If there are priests among us, then there are also kings among us. In the Old Testament era, kings were rulers over territories and kingdoms. In today's world, kings could be monarchs over a geo-political area. Or in Rich Marshall's concept, they could be successful business owners.

Think about it—they have a realm of rule; they prosper due to God's favor on their career or vocation; they have a sphere of influence with people in certain defined borders; they start up new businesses, and become producers of wealth for themselves and other people.

These "Economic Kings" oversee a domain of business

or merchandising due to their God-given talent and divine opportunities. Indeed, the meek shall inherit the earth, and the righteous will be blessed.

In the kingdom of God, they can use their wealth, not just for self-serving purposes, but to extend the gospel and to support the mission of the church. They are like Dr. Luke, the businessman who traveled with the apostle Paul. They are the rich men whom Paul exhorted to lay up treasure in heaven by generosity on earth. They team up with God's servants to help the gospel advance. They are a resource base for those who devote themselves to the ministry of the word and prayer. We need them for the church to succeed.

By God's grace, they have the grace-gift of giving. Without them and their liberality, the church would be greatly hampered in its efforts to spread the gospel. Which are you—a king or a priest? You may be both!

Too many Christians despise their work. They think if they are not serving full-time in the ministry, then their life doesn't count for much. This is wrong thinking and a sad attitude. We should realize that meaningful work is a gift from a loving God. All that we do—in church, in society, or in our family, should be done as unto the Lord. *We serve God* with our work, not just our company or customers or our boss. We should work whole-heartedly, knowing the Lord is watching.

Whether the church structure is facility-based or cell-based, there will always be a need for someone to give their undivided attention to the work of the Word and the spiritual care of the people. That worker will need to be supported in a way that agrees with the Bible. We will never do away with the need for giving to God se we can support the workers whom he has called.

People have funny ways of trying to get around these principles. Some church boards are afraid they'll pay their pastor too much. They say, "He's not in it for the money; we don't need to give him any more than the bare minimum." Really?

This not only takes unfair advantage of a man with pure motives, but it also demeans him and treats him like a hireling. This is the opposite of what Jesus said—that the laborer is worthy of his wages. He (or she) should be respected.

Stingy church boards don't realize that when they pay lean wages to their pastor, they are spreading a spirit of poverty throughout the whole church. *"There is that scattereth, and yet increaseth; and there is that withholdeth more than is meet, but it tendeth to poverty. The liberal soul shall be made fat: and he that watereth shall be watered also himself"* (Proverbs 11:24-25 KJV).

Don't withhold what is due. God is watching. He will render a just verdict upon all who sow leanness into the flock.

Anyone who chokes off the supply of finances to God's worker needs to walk in the fear of an angry God. If you withhold what is due, you will be made lean yourself. If you look for ways to be generous, God will be liberal with you. God doesn't expect anyone to do more than they are able, but he does expect us to be generous with what we have.

Generosity isn't something to postpone until the future. You can't afford to withhold what is due. "Do not withhold good from those who deserve it, when it is in your power to act. Do not say to your neighbor, 'Come back later; I'll give it tomorrow'-- when you now have it with you." (Prov. 3:27-28 NIV)

God sees your procrastination and starts reducing your supply. Fear of the future can be a self-fulfilling prophecy. Instead, have faith that if you sow now, you will reap more later. Through having faith and endurance we inherit the promises. One of my favorite declarations when I give is, *"There's more where that came from!"*

Reasonable Salaries

How do you establish a full-time pastor's salary? One way would be to see what other professional people in your area with similar years of education, training, or experience are being paid.

I have noticed that my pay scale as a pastor in a well-established church, when I wasn't sacrificially starting a new work or repairing a small struggling church, seemed comparable to that of a math teacher with a master's degree after 25 years of service, which I have now passed. But the math teacher had additional benefits like a retirement program, paid vacation, promotional incentives, and health insurance, etc. Ironically, janitors in New York City schools make more than the teachers. I suppose the janitors have a stronger union.

Here is another way to get an idea of how a pastor may be fairly paid—take an average income of all the professional workers who are heads of households in the church, then pay that average figure as a salary, plus a little extra besides. Why the extra? In the Bible, the Levites received tithes from eleven other tribes, making their income 10% above all the other tribes. God is generous with his servants. Of course, the responsibility which a leader carries should also affect his salary level. How valuable is he or she to the organization? Is he really a key man? How many years has he invested in the work? How fruitful is his ministry?

Because of the restoration taking place in the church, we are now learning not only how to support local pastors, but how churches can sponsor apostles (missionaries) and prophets (reformers). In fact, let me make a bold statement which only the passage of time will verify. Due to the urgent priority of the ripening harvest and the desperate need for laborers to be trained, it will become increasingly important that apostles and prophets be sent out and fully funded.

In other words, *advancing the mission* will become equally important as *maintaining the status quo.*

Concluding Cautions

ANY TIME YOU DEAL with money, you touch a sensitive subject that can either bless folks or hurt people depending on how this truth is applied. For example, what about preachers who take this doctrine regarding money and deliver it in a heavy-handed way? What about charlatans on TV who offer God's gifts for money? Stay away from these phonies. I've seen the results of greed. I've proven the principle in my own life: if you won't serve God for freed, then you should not serve God for money. Don't be a hireling in motivation. Keep your heart free of greed. At the same time, God is righteous to remember you and reward you. God wants to prosper his workers.

I dread the prospect of abuse. Yet I know some religious leaders will take this very truth designed to be a blessing and apply it in a demanding, manipulative, controlling way. That legalistic approach puts people into bondage. Paul warned us in 2 Cor. 3:6, *"the letter kills, but the Spirit gives life."*

Truth ministered in the Spirit, based on love and faith,

builds up and empowers believers. It is liberating! Truth ministered in harshness and legalism produces condemnation and causes bondage. *We cannot turn God's word of faith into a word of law, devoid of grace.* Instead, people should experience the glorious liberty of obedience based on their growing faith in God's eternal word. Be gentle with the poor and ignorant. Be patient with those undergoing strange trials or tests. Instruct the people. You can't rightly hold people accountable to something that they have never been taught. Lead by example. Teach precepts.

Leaders of the church ought not trespass on someone's conscience and demand their obedience in an area where they have not yet come to faith or understanding. Right teaching of good doctrine must precede accountability.

Giving is between an individual and God. God respects a person's convictions and so should we. People need time to learn and to respond. Teachers and pastors must feed their flocks with knowledge and lead them into the truth in a loving and patient manner. The Bible should be taught in word and deed. We should set an example for our followers.

Let me say a few words about pastors and how they should deal with this issue. There are some definite pitfalls to avoid. God wants us to offer truth that sets people free. God doesn't want his people to feel beaten and condemned. *Meek messengers feed the sheep. Tough ramrods drive the herd.* How the word is delivered affects how it will be received. The messenger who delivers the truth must have already been under the dealings of God. This is called the "Desert Principle."

Moses spent forty years in the wilderness before he was sufficiently humbled for God to use him in a significant way. Paul was persecuted for years before he began to fulfill his full apostolic calling. Jesus was under submission to his natural parents and to Jewish law for thirty years before he was ready for three years of public miraculous ministry.

A Thief in the Storehouse

God wants foundational ministry to come from seasoned fathers in the faith. Young "Joshua" ministers can go to war to deliver the people but only mature "Moses" leaders can guide and govern the flock.

Sometimes the zeal of our youth causes us to rush ahead, not realizing we are leaving the flock behind. Thankfully, God tempers us with age and experience, increasing our wisdom.

We see in the Bible that God invests a great deal of time in preparing his servant so he or she can handle the Lord's people righteously. God not only trains them in his word, but he also deals with their heart and their motivations. Genuine leaders have lived under authority, they have served, they have had their dreams dashed and tested, and hopefully they have become corporate and accountable. Their character has become Christ-like. Their words minister life. Who they are speaks as just as loudly as what they say.

A Christian or minister who has not been brought to the cross and seen the end of his own pride and or human ability is not ready to lead God's people or exercise authority. An anointed messenger, apart from the cross, only displays proud flesh. Un-crucified carnality, even if it is anointed of the Holy Spirit, still smells like decaying flesh.

The cross is God's solution to selfish ambition and mixed motives. At the foot of the cross, we lay down our lives to obey God and become able to bless his people. We are given grace to walk in love. Preachers must sacrificially love the people to whom they are sent or else they are disqualified from speaking anything in God's house.

God has built into his kingdom certain safeguards. These safeguards are activated through various trials which purify our motives. Our God is a wise master builder. He wants to use building materials in his house which have first been proven and have passed his rigorous test. No defective bricks or beams; no substandard wiring or plumbing! Since God builds with people, that means he puts his chosen servants through the hottest fire.

Posture before Position

The greater the degree of grace, anointing or authority which someone in the ministry is destined to carry, the hotter the fire of preparation time they will have to endure. If they fail the test, they are demoted, delayed, or cast aside. This rule is obvious in both the Old Testament and the New Testament.

God put Moses, his choice prophet, through misunderstanding, persecution, and forty years of protracted servitude in the wilderness before revealing his glory to him and calling him to deliver his people from Egypt. When God finished with Moses, he was the meekest man on the face of the earth. His anger and ambition were (almost) dead.

Proven character qualifies leaders to handle the gold and the glory, money and applause. It gives them gentleness and wisdom in their style of leadership. If leaders bypass this phase of preparation, they self-destruct and damage the church.

One safeguard is this— only ministers with a true shepherd's heart are entitled to live off the wool of their flock. The ministry is not something you call yourself into. *If you won't do it without pay, you shouldn't get to do it for pay.* Jesus described genuine shepherds in John 10 as those being willing to lay down their lives for the sheep.

This willingness to serve, sacrifice, and suffer for the flock is opposite to the nature of a wolf. A wolf devours the flock and feeds his own appetites. If a preacher is greedy for gain, he is not qualified to live off his ministry. (This topic is addressed strongly in Ezekiel 34.)

Preachers who get into the ministry just to have a job will eventually fail and be cast aside, as well they should. No one should make the mistake of thinking that they can call themselves into the ministry.

Grace is free. Everything we have, we received as a gift from God. No one can extract a fee for the gospel or its benefits. No leader can demand honor—that must be earned. No prophet should demand to be paid for his prophecies. We can't merchandise the gospel. If we do, we become charlatans, condemned like Balaam, the false prophet who uttered true words, but did it for money.

What was false about him? *His motives. He could be bought!* Our service is a free gift to God and to his people.

Simon the sorcerer, a convert to Christ, was severely reprimanded for approaching the things of God with greedy motives (Acts 8:20). No one can merchandise the gifts of the Holy Spirit. They are gifts of grace. It is a privilege to minister our gifts for God. If you get paid for it, that's God's prerogative, not yours. Servants don't ask what their salary will be, because they have no rights. They are owned by their master. Fortunately, our Master treats his servants well.

When a shepherd has this attitude in his heart, then God can begin to trust him or her with income derived from the flock they serve. God enforces this character test by having ministers labor at their own expense or serve as an apprentice without pay while under another man's ministry before they have the privilege of living off the tithe themselves. This is for their preparation and proving.

On the other hand, it is unrighteous and wicked for a church board or eldership or a presbytery to withhold what is due when it is in their power to pay it. It is wrong for a church to invite a guest minister to speak, take up offerings for them, then pay them a pittance while pocketing the rest.

This is stealing! It disregards their needs, the distance they came, the years of preparation they have invested, and it dishonors the Lord who sent them.

Nor should a church council or congregation take advantage of a minister's devotion to his calling by paying him or her as little as they possibly can. This is stingy and greedy and does not reflect the attitude of the Lord of the Harvest toward his laborers. For this reason, many pastors' kids reject the idea of following their father into the ministry, having seen how their family was mistreated and poorly paid.

The Lord is watching not only the motives of his leaders, but also the motives of the members of the church who provide for them or handle church administration.

A *spirit of control* often comes over a church when it comes time to deliberate on budget items involving salaries. Beware of this. At best this is carnality. At worst it is a type of witchcraft. The love of money is a root of all sorts of evil (1 Tim. 6:10). Shepherds must avoid the wrong motive of being eager for sordid profit (1 Peter 5:2) and boards of churches must avoid any hint of stinginess or greed.

Liberality and faithfulness is a shield against covetousness. Knowing God's word regarding finances will keep us on track. Honoring God with tithes and helping the needy with offerings will protect us from greed. Giving freely as a lifestyle attracts abundant grace from God.

God requires leaders to live a lifestyle of obedience in finances before they begin to teach this. Obedience precedes abundance. A budget enables generosity. In my mind, this includes one practical area often neglected: *Freedom from debt.* Many a man of God has forfeited his leadership because he could not afford to take a righteous stand for the truth due to the risk of losing his paycheck. Of course, that makes him a hireling. We must be examples kingdom economics in sound family finances and in our personal giving.

I have found that pastors who practice honoring God with their own tithes and offerings rarely have trouble leading their flock into this same practice. People resent being pushed but they are certainly willing to be led.

Seven Summary Statements

WHEN GOD GOES AFTER the errors or the sins that restrict his glory and hurt our lives, he does so with irrefutable evidence. It is important that the word be laid out clearly and that motives remain pure. Therefore, let me state my conclusions and add some wise precautions.

1) *The tithe belongs to those set apart for the ministry.* Failure to release the tithe to God's servants can cause a curse to rest on a person or a church. The tithe enables gospel workers to be supported so the word can be taught to God's people. Gospel workers are supported by the tithes of God's faithful people, so they can give themselves to prayer, to the word, and to spend time with the people they are training.

Any church board that covets the tithes for its own agenda, and defrauds the worker, is guilty of sin just the same as any man coveting another man's wife.

2) *Subverting the use of the tithe for any other purpose is dangerous.* In the business realm, we call this misappropriation of funds. In the kingdom of God, the Bible

calls it stealing. The apostles called it defrauding the worker of his wages. Leaders gifted with governmental grace and called to the ministry should handle the tithe. Why? Because it is sanctified for this exact use. This is the system ordained by the Lord all throughout the Bible. In God's house, the fathers in the faith should set the budget. If they delegate this responsibility, those doing so must act as stewards who give an account, never as owners.

3) *Tithing (paying God the first 10% of our income) is the beginning of obedience in finances.* It has a promise of blessings from God, *if* we bring the whole tithe into the storehouse. Tithing permits us to get into the realm of offerings, which is giving beyond the initial first fruit. Tithing fulfills our obligation to honor God, but giving is an act of love. Giving beyond our tithe lets us sow and reap. Giving extra (for missions, for buildings, to send out workers, to help the needy) has a promise of great increase and enlargement in God. We tithe to get the curse off our money, then we give so we can realize abundance.

4) *Tithing honors God.* It is a tangible act of worship. We worship God with our material wealth when we give to him first. The tithe goes to God before anything else. Our affections are kept in proper order when we invest in God above all other things. God honors those who honor him. Jesus is pictured in Revelation as worthy of receiving wealth as well as worship.

5) *The love of money incites idolatry.* Money also causes contests over control. Remember: whoever controls the money controls the church. The Bible has a great deal to say about how to receive, direct, and expend the finances of the church. The apostles gave explicit instructions for how churches were to support ministers. The apostles placed control of the church's money in the hands of God's appointed leadership, the shepherding elders of the church. They knew God wanted his portion from the field he had

planted, watered, and sent workers into. Pastors and elders of local churches also need to guard against greed and not think that God's blessings on their work is all just for themselves. They need to participate in supporting missionaries, apostles, and other traveling leaders.

6) *Ignorance over handling money causes chaos and missed opportunities.* Carnal systems have been invented in churches because preachers misused the tithe or because power-hungry people tried to dominate the ministers. God is restoring a biblical mandate for handling finances concurrent with the restoration of apostles and prophets. The foundations for prosperity in God's house are being rediscovered. The keys to restoration are being given to teachers who have embraced the cross, not a personal success formula, who want to do God's will. At the same time, transitions in established churches take time and require wisdom to enact without splitting the wineskin.

7) *Because of sin and because of abuses, there will always be a necessity for a system of accountability to cover those called into the ministry.* Shepherds need to watch over each other. Every leader needs someone who is not afraid to tell him (or her) the truth. Financial extravagance is a sin equivalent to gluttony. Pastors need to be related to other pastors and to ministry teams. Accountability is essential. Spiritual fathers or overseers need to guard their spheres lest greed gain a foothold.

Prosperity has its own unique set of temptations. Power can corrupt the naive or the arrogant. Novices need supervision. Humility and team leadership can help us avoid pitfalls when we lack necessary skills. Pastors should not hesitate to call on the expertise of trained individuals who can advise them and render assistance in practical areas. Headship responsibility demands that some parts of the work be delegated to trustworthy servants. The church needs to have confidence that their leaders are getting wise counsel and exercising good stewardship.

Sons can't easily hold their fathers accountable, yet the whole family of faith must be able to see and imitate the virtues of leadership. These virtues include walking in the light, willingness to admit mistakes, ability to receive correction, honesty in all things, and functioning in moral and financial integrity.

Financial integrity is manifested by a disciplined lifestyle, freedom from covetousness, a good bookkeeping system that is both legal and efficient, trustworthy stewardship proven over time, and a heart of generosity toward church staff, the nearby poor, and toward foreign missions.

Generosity is revealed by an attitude of eagerness to give resources away from yourself into opportunities that will reap dividends for the kingdom, even if not directly benefitting your own church or sphere of ministry. Richard Stearns, President of World Vision, says in his book, *The Hole in our Gospel*, that we must use charity to help the poor in the name of Christ.

The hearts of genuine apostles and pastors in the first century church displayed a godly desire to bless the poor, not only with the gospel, but also with charity. We all must do this as well. When finances become abundant, it is just as wasteful to consume them all upon ourselves as it is to become a glutton when food is plentiful.

The Wages of an Apostle

LOCAL PASTORS in established churches have an accepted and recognized pattern of receiving salaries, supporting their families, and earning a livelihood. The question is, do the other five-fold ministries of Christ deserve to be supported as well? Is there a practical way to do this?

God viewed as robbery his peoples' failure to support the priests in the Old Testament (Mal. 3:6-12). How do you think he views our failure to support Jesus' modern apostles, prophets, evangelists, or teachers in the new covenant? If the Lord said to pray for more workers for the harvest, what will happen if we *pray,* but do not *pay?*

In real life, this is how the economy works: whatever task you provide good compensation for, you will get more workers for that task. It is a practical reality. If you pay pastors, you will get more pastors. What if you pay prophets? Or apostles? Where does their remuneration come from? We cannot neglect this point of concern.

If this topic is important—and it is— then certainly the Lord would give us clear instructions, right? Well, the Lord has done exactly that. A surprising number of different scriptures address this very issue.

I want to focus on one passage, found in 1 Corinthians

9, written by the apostle Paul. I have already quoted this passage previously in this book. Now let's revisit it. Here is Paul's appeal to the Corinthian church, a colony of heaven that he himself established. Based on his relationship with them, he argued the case for his right for financial honor.

Am I not free? Am I not an apostle? Have I not seen Jesus our Lord? Are you not my work in the Lord? If to others I am not an apostle, at least I am to you; for you are the seal of my apostleship in the Lord. My defense to those who examine me is this: Do we not have a right to eat and drink? Do we not have a right to take along a believing wife, even as the rest of the apostles and the brothers of the Lord and Cephas?

Or do only Barnabas and I not have a right to refrain from working? Who at any time serves as a soldier at his own expense? Who plants a vineyard and does not eat the fruit of it? Or who tends a flock and does not use the milk of the flock? I am not speaking these things according to human judgment, am I? Or does not the Law also say these things? For it is written in the Law of Moses, "You shall not muzzle the ox while he is threshing." God is not concerned about oxen, is He? Or is He speaking altogether for our sake? Yes, for our sake it was written, because the plowman ought to plow in hope, and the thresher to thresh in hope of sharing the crops.

If we sowed spiritual things in you, is it too much if we reap material things from you? If others share the right over you, do we not more?

Nevertheless, we did not use this right, but we endure all things so that we will cause no hindrance to the gospel of Christ. Do you not know that those who perform sacred services eat the food of the temple, and those who attend regularly to the altar have their share from the altar?

So also, the Lord directed those who proclaim the gospel to get their living from the gospel. (1 Cor. 9:1-14 NASB)

In reading familiar portions of scripture, we may fly

right past a verse because we think we already know what it means. Often, the Lord invites us to slow down and reconsider, to think in a new way with him, to comprehend what he is saying to us in his word.

God has ideas and ways that are higher than our old opinions or traditional paradigms (Is. 55:8-9). Follow along with me as I break out the ideas found in 1 Corinthians 9, phrase by phrase, in these divinely inspired verses written and recorded as foundational church truth. They were relevant to Corinth in that day and they remain relevant to us in our day.

Verse 1

Am I not free? Why would the apostle Paul say "free?" What was he free of? He was free of the Law. The "apostle of grace" was now living by faith in Christ. He was free of the temple system that depended on offerings being brought into a temple or a religious building. He was free of a secular vocation tying him down to one spot. He was able to travel and move about with his fellow workers, all of which required a lot of money for their expenses.

Am I not an apostle? Paul carried the identifying marks of a genuine apostle. He said, *"The signs of a true apostle were performed among you with all perseverance, by signs and wonders and miracles."* (2 Cor 12:12 NASB) Not only did Paul have the supernatural credentials by gifts of the Holy Spirit, he also displayed perseverance. In 1 Corinthians 11-12, he detailed the extraordinary suffering and trials that he had endured for the sake of his apostolic ministry. One thing about apostles is this: *they don't quit!*

Have I not seen Jesus our Lord? This was remarkable because Paul was saved and called to serve the Lord *after* the resurrection and ascension of Jesus. He had never seen Jesus in the flesh, only by visions or by the Spirit. Jesus had appeared to Paul on the road to Damascus. Paul was a notable "post-Ascension" apostle of Christ, one of at least a dozen identified in the New Testament *after* Jesus returned to heaven, in addition to the original Twelve. All apostles carry an awesome revelation of Jesus in their heart and mind. Some, like the apostle Paul, have seen the risen Lord.

Are you not my work in the Lord? He was like a shepherd saying, "You are my sheep and I am your shepherd." Paul was saying he had a right to make a living from his flock. Like a farmer laying claim to the produce of his own fields, he had a relationship with the church in Corinth. He had evangelized them. He was their spiritual father. He had made disciples there. He had grounded their faith in God's power. He had first proclaimed the gospel to them. As their apostle, he had priority with them.

Verse 2

*"You are **the seal** of my apostleship in the Lord."* Paul claimed a relationship with them that no one else could claim—he was their founding apostle. They were in debt to him. He was not an apostle to the world, but he was to them. Paul was *their* apostle. Giving to him financially would reflect his legitimate right, thus recognizing his apostolic work among them. They were the proof of his apostleship.

A genuine apostle produces fruit that only an apostle's ministry can produce: a new church that is set in order and can reproduce. The church at Corinth was the evidence (the seal, the stamp of authenticity) that Paul was a genuine apostle. While a pastor may feed or shepherd an established congregation, an apostle can start from scratch with nobody, and by God's grace, raise up a fully-functioning colony of heaven, an *eclessia*, a covenant community in which God dwells by his Spirit.

Verse 3

Paul invited them to **examine him.** He had offered abundant evidence that he was *their* apostle. In this context, he was entitled to be supported financially by the Corinthian church. This was important because false or counterfeit apostles ("super-apostles") were circulating who were taking from the churches. Paul undercut those imposters by sacrificially serving the gospel to Corinth at no charge, thus proving he loved them like a father. The false apostles used the title "apostle" but they were takers, not givers. Jesus commended the church for examining and discrediting false apostles (Rev. 2:2).

Verses 4-6

Paul offers a list of things in his **defense.** *"Do we not have a right to eat and drink?"* That is obvious. Anyone doing the work is worthy of his wages. Jesus had stated this to those he sent out. (see Luke 10:1-12) *"Do we not have a right to take along a believing wife?"* By being devoted to the ministry, by working to expand the sphere of the gospel and by being mobile to do it, they sacrificed the ability to pursue a career. If they were married and had a family, they deserved to be provided for as well. A minister's family ought not to feel deprived just because they are in the business of serving God's people. Paul said this pattern was already in place for the other apostles and brothers of the Lord and for Cephas (Peter).

Do we not *"have a right to refrain from working?"* He and Barnabas were on the road with their travelling apostolic ministry. As such, they had the right to forego secular employment. They needed to be devoted to the word and to prayer. They need to be fully supported by the people they were serving. Paul called this "a right." Not only was it a right, it often was a practical necessity for his success.

Verse 7

What soldier goes to war at his own expense? No one leaves home and marches off to war without two things: 1) the authority of the government commissioning and sending him; 2) all the material provisions that would be needed for safety and victory. In Paul's day, Roman legions were the world's finest and fiercest fighting machines. John the Baptist said to soldiers who came to him, "Be content with your wages." Soldiers going into battle have wages. Apostles are God's generals on the front lines.

Who plants a vineyard? Any farmer who plants and cultivates a vineyard fully expects to partake of the crop. **Who tends a flock?** Paul used the example of a shepherd caring for sheep. That shepherd had the perfect right to sell the wool or eat the meat. He made his living off the sheep.

Verse 8

Paul appeals to the **pattern of God's word.** We need to know what the Bible has to say. Jesus said the scriptures cannot be broken. The word has many examples and precepts that teach us how to support God's servants. It all begins with honor but then must become practical.

Verse 9

Don't muzzle the ox. The laborer who produces the bounty for its master is the ox. Any owner of oxen knows that when an ox is grinding the grain, he needs to eat to keep working. Businessmen in the world know that to motivate their employees, there must be faithful remuneration and a system of rewarding those who are more productive. If you strangle the money supply of God's workers, you will demotivate them, hurt the harvest, and defraud God.

Verse 10

Plow in hope; thresh in hope. This is written in the word of God. This addresses the heart motivation. Even David, as he faced Goliath, asked, "What was the reward?" He was zealous for God's name, but he was also motivated to achieve an earthly double reward: a wife and freedom from taxation. Laborers need to know there is hope of a tangible reward. Not all pay is waiting in heaven. Apostles need to eat and provide for their family now, on the earth.

Verse 11

Sowing and Reaping. God has built into the universe a law of payback, a cycle of reciprocity. What you sow, you will reap, just more of it. Every living seed has an ability to multiply based on the life that is in it. First the natural, then the spiritual. The seed is the word. Paul asserted the right to reap material things (financial support) based on sowing spiritual things (the word, faith, grace, truth, his life as an example, *pneumatikos*) into the lives of people hearing him.

Verse 12

We do not use this right. Other people had been supported by the Corinthian church. Even more so, Paul deserved to be supported. However, he did not use this right on certain occasions. This unusual behavior doesn't make yielding his right a pattern, but rather it was the exception. He explained in detail why he did this—to undercut false apostles. (pseudo-apostles – see 2 Cor. 11:7-13; 12:11)

Verse 13

Those who serve the altar live from the altar. Priests in the temple displayed the pattern of consuming offerings brought by the people to the Lord. This is another pattern that Paul appealed to, and it is a powerful argument.

Verse 14

Finally, Paul's defense of his right to be supported as an apostle (*i.e.*- "sent one") is this: he appeals to **the highest authority**, the Lord Jesus Christ. *"The Lord directed those who proclaim the gospel to get their living from the gospel."*

The End

Author's prayer

This book is intended for the good of the body of Christ and for the glory of my Lord. I offer this concluding prayer- *"Remember me for this, O my God, and do not blot out what I have so faithfully done for the house of my God and its services."* (Neh. 13:14)

A Thief in the House © 2018 by Ron Wood. Previously published as *The Thief in the Storehouse* © Copyright 1999-2017 by Ronald E. Wood. All rights reserved.

Biblical References

KJV scriptures from the *King James Version* of the Holy Bible. **NIV** from *The Holy Bible: The New International Version*, by the International Bible Society, by Zondervan Bible Publishers, Grand Rapids, Michigan. **NASB** from the *New American Standard Bible, Updated Version*, by The Lockman Foundation, La Habra, CA. **NKJV** from the *New King James Version, Holy Bible*, Thomas Nelson, Inc., Nashville, TN. Original language references are from *The Strong's Exhaustive Concordance*, pub. by Thomas Nelson Publishers, Nashville, TN.

About the Author

Ron and his wife, Lana, have been pastors in Baptist, Covenant, and Assembly of God churches and served as missionaries in South Africa. He is a graduate of Southeastern University with a degree in Missions. Ron teaches the Bible with humor, prophetic insight, and practical application. He is a writer with hundreds of newspaper articles published and is the author of several books. Lana is a fourth-generation Christian minister. They have two children and six grandchildren and live in NW Arkansas.

Ron is available for presentations, forums, and seminars. To inquire about his ministry in your church or conference, contact: www.touchedbygrace.org.

Partner with us

Touched by Grace is a US based non-profit 501-c-3. We provide training materials for development of a Christian world-view, the Reformation of the church, tools for equipping the next generation, and we offer humanitarian and educational assistance in strategic locations as an NGO.

Ministry Resources
Website: www.touchedbygrace.org
Facebook: @touchedbygracenwa
Email: ron@touchedbygrace.org
Subscribe: Free Newsletter, Articles, Coming Events

Classes: Webinars and Online Training Courses

Workshops: (by TBG Team Members)
   Hearing God's Voice – the gift of prophecy today
   Power Evangelism – authority to heal diseases
   Deliverance Team Protocol – things to know and do
   How to Have a Healing Ministry in a Local Church
   Church Government & Growth – analyze & discuss
   Identifying Emerging Apostles and Prophets

BOOKS by Ron Wood Available for order at Amazon.com or other online retailers in paperback, or e-books for Kindle or other e-reader devices. *Indicates Spanish versions are available.

*Women on the Team

Why did Paul have so many women on his apostolic team? The Lord calls women into ministry and full leadership in the church. This examination reveals that women can do anything the Holy Spirit anoints them to do.

*A Thief in the Storehouse

The devil wants to choke our churches with poverty. But the Lord is transforming financial traditions to bless the saints and empower churches or ministry teams. As we prosper, our mission is to complete the Great Commission.

*Houses of Prayer in the City

How do pastors and intercessors work together? How do churches in a city unite in prayer to defeat Satan and evangelize their region with the gospel's power? Why is warfare prayer the number one priority of the church?

Emerging Apostles in the Developing Church

The church has become something the Lord didn't intend. We try programs to make it grow but God is looking for the person who has encountered King Jesus. Are you an emerging apostle in the developing church?

Deliverance - Our Legacy

Discover how Jesus liberated people who were troubled by evil spirits, giving them joy *and* freedom. Learn how you can use deliverance to minister healing to yourself or others in a biblical, beneficial, balanced, and wise way.

The Riches of God's Grace

Legalism is a polite way of backsliding. The Law produces religious performance and guilt while Grace produces rest through believing. No personal foundation is more important than faith in the finished work of Christ.

The New Joseph Season

God is creating a covenant of blessing between believers in business and ministry teams that are exporting God's word. The end-time transfer of wealth has begun.

Heaven's Angel Army

What happens when believers line up with God's will and pray heaven down on earth? What moves God's powerful holy angels to act on behalf of the saints? Learn how mighty angels cooperate with intercessors as the Holy Spirit inspires us to prophesy and proclaim God's will.

Damaged by Adult ADD

If an adult in your family has *undiagnosed* ADD (Attention Deficit Disorder), it needs to be professionally treated. How do you cope? Read my personal story and learn practical skills that people have used to moderate ADD's damaging effects on their life, marriage, career, and family.

Powerful Fathers

America suffers from an epidemic of disappearing dads. Where have all the fathers gone? How do we raise a new generation of boys who learn how to behave like men? (Unlike the previous book, *Tales from a Father,* this version includes study questions for groups, with Scripture verses.)

Made in the USA
Coppell, TX
20 February 2026

71777237R00079